Dream Catchers

Developing Career and Educational Awareness in the Intermediate Grades

Reproducible Activity Sheets

Norene Lindsay

from JIST the job search people

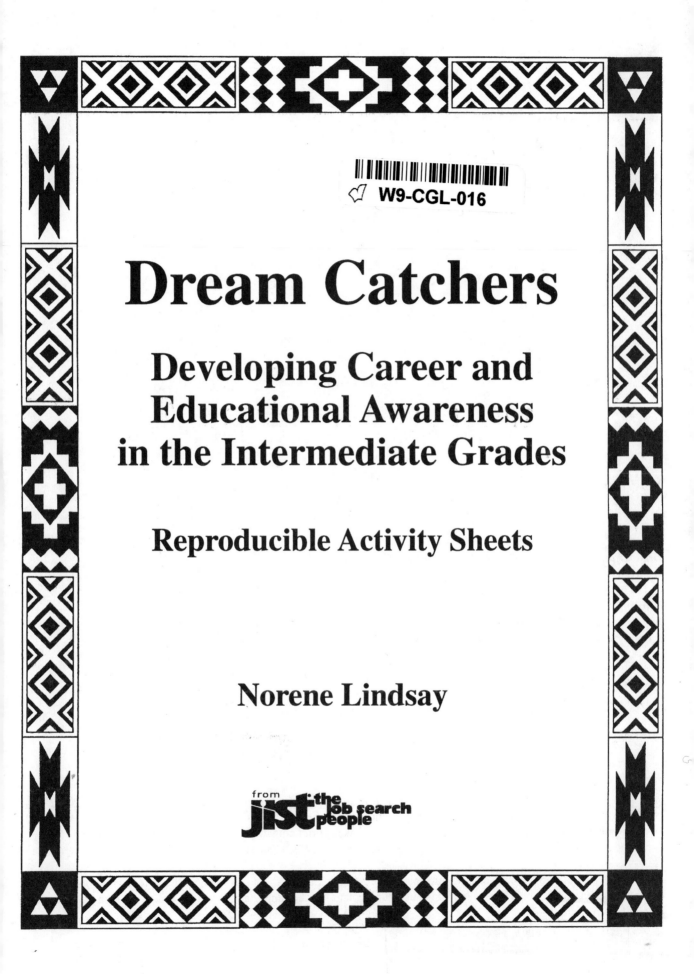

Dream Catchers—Reproducible Activity Sheet Workbook
Reorder #4015

720 N. Park Avenue
Indianapolis, IN 46202-3431
Phone: 317-264-3720 **Fax:** 317-264-3709 **E-mail:** JISTWorks@AOL.com

Cover Design by Inter Con, Inc. and Dean Johnson Design Group
Illustrations by Michael Gurtzweiler

Printed in the United States of America

99 98 97 96 5 4 3 2 1

ISBN: 1-56370-087-5

Preface

Schools nationwide have recognized the need to emphasize career awareness programs in the intermediate grades. This emphasis makes good sense because of the increasingly competitive global economy, the changing nature of work, and the importance of education and career planning to a student's success as an adult.

Specific guidelines for career awareness competencies at the intermediate level have been developed by the National Occupational Information Coordinating Committee (NOICC). Many school systems are attempting to implement NOICC's guidelines, but few educational materials have been designed for this purpose. The *Dream Catchers* books are one of the first to be written specifically to fulfill NOICC guidelines.

A great advantage of the *Dream Catchers* materials is that they can be integrated into any academic subject or can be used as a separate, complete career awareness curriculum. The reproducible activity sheets in this book are all coded for easy integration into your classroom work. They will allow you to expand and enhance career awareness concepts plus strengthen academic skills as well.

Table of Contents

Introduction

Additional Photocopies 1
Organization 1
Codes 2
Reproductions 2
Flexibility 2

PART 1: Capture Your Dreams—*The Choice Is Yours*

1. Write a Letter Home 5
2. Make Your Own Dream Catcher 7
3. Make Your Own Cluster Games 9
4. Career Cluster Collages 11
5. Agriculture and Natural Resource Cluster Worksheet 13
6. Business and Marketing Cluster Worksheet 15
7. Communications, Art, and Design Cluster Worksheet 17
8. Construction and Production Cluster Worksheet 19
9. Education, Human Services, and Personal Service Cluster Worksheet 21
10. Health Cluster Worksheet 23
11. Repairers and Mechanics Cluster Worksheet 25
12. Science and Technology Cluster Worksheet 27
13. Transportation Cluster Worksheet 29
14. You Work with People and Animals Too! 31
15. You Work with Things and Machinery Too! 33
16. You Work with Data Too! 35
17. Discovering More Working Conditions.. 37
18. Conduct a Work Force Survey 39
19. Career Data Worksheet 41
20. Write a Letter Requesting Career Information 43
21. Careers of Famous People 45
22. Make a Career Cluster Handbook 47
23. Plan a Job Fair 49
24. Write a Wild Work Story! 51
25. Pick Your "Dream" Career 53
26. What's My Line? 55
27. Work in Early America 57
28. Inventions Create Jobs! 59
29. Jobs of the Future 61
30. Job Genealogy 63
31. Workplaces in Your Community 65
32. Volunteer Work in Your Community 67
33. Plan a Class Volunteer Project 69
34. Write a Letter Home—Part 1 71

PART 2: The Stuff Dreams Are Made Of—*Discovering Your Skills*

35. Make a Skills Chain 75
36. Make a Skills Bank 77
37. Share Your Skills 79
38. You Can Be an Apprentice 81
39. Practice Makes Perfect 83
40. What Academic Skills Are Needed for Jobs? 85
41. Using Your Academic Skills Outside of School 87
42. Using Your Self-Management Skills 89
43. Improving Your Self-Management Skills 91
44. Using Time Efficiently in the Workplace 93
45. Make a School Timecard 95
46. The Case of the "Bad Worker" 97
47. What Job-Related Skills Do You Need? . 99
48. Create a Job-Related Skills Bulletin Board 101
49. Using the Want Ads to Learn About Skills 103
50. Write a Letter Home—Part 2 105

PART 3: Making Dreams Come True—*Ability, Effort, and Achievement*

51. Produce a "Three Little Pigs" Play 109
52. You Can Improve Too! 111
53. My Time Journal 113
54. How You Use Your Time 115
55. Setting Achievement Goals 117
56. Make a Schoolwork Planner 119
57. Managing Your School Study Time 121
58. Using School Study Time Better 123
59. "A Test Is Coming!" 125
60. Learn from Your Mistakes 127
61. My Workplace Plan 129
62. Organizing an Efficient Workplace 131
63. Improving Your School Workplace 133
64. Developing a Job Chart 135
65. Write a Letter Home—Part 3 137

PART 4: Putting Your Dreams to Work—*Work and the Needs and Functions of Society*

66. Why Do People Work? 141
67. Why Do You Work? 143
68. Work and Society 145
69. What Would Happen If 147
70. On Strike! 149
71. What Are Goods and Services? 151
72. Services for Your Home 153
73. Where Do Goods Come From? 155
74. The Global Economy 157
75. Goods from Around the World 159

Introduction

This "reproducible activity sheets book" contains 75 activities that can be easily removed for duplication and supplementation of the *Dream Catchers* student activity book.

The activities are designed to enhance and expand the concepts explored in the student activity book. The *Dream Catchers Teacher's Guide* will give you complete instructions on how to easily integrate the activities into your lesson plans.

While we believe you would benefit from the helpful information found in the teacher's guide, it is not essential for use with the reproducibile activity sheets.

Additional Photocopies

The activity sheets in this book are designed specifically for use with the consumable student activity book of the same name—*Dream Catchers.* If you are using *Dream Catchers* as a student text for classroom purposes, you are hereby authorized to make additional photocopies from this book as needed.

Organization

The activities are organized numerically to correspond to the three parts of the *Dream Catchers* book as you will see in the Table of Contents. A fourth section on activities that relate to "Work and the Needs and Functions of Society" has also been included if you choose to pursue that topic.

Codes

Each activity sheet has a code in the upper right hand corner. The codes tell you how this activity can be used with your students. The codes are as follows:

"I"— This code stands for "individual." It designates that the activity can be performed by the student alone. You may choose to have the whole class do an "I" activity at the same time, but they can also be done independently.

"SG"— This code stands for "small group." It designates that the activity can be performed in small groups. Some "SG" activities require the use of small groups while others have the option of the student performing the activity independently.

"C"— This code stands for "class." It designates that the activity will require participation by the whole class for at least part of the activity.

"2 Pages"— A few of the activity sheets contain instructions that take up two pages. When that occurs, the code "2 Pages" appears also.

Reproductions

Some of the activity sheets are reproductions of pages in the *Dream Catchers* book. These pages are reproduced because you may have use for more than one. You might, for example, want your students to take home some of their goal-setting exercises to share with their parent(s) or guardian(s), or if you have them research more than one career for instance, you will need to reproduce more "Career Data Worksheets."

The teacher's guide will always indicate if a particular page in *Dream Catchers* is available in the reproducible activity sheets. The activity sheets which are reproductions from the book include numbers 19, 52, 53, 55, and 61. The activity sheets also contain a sheet representing each career cluster. These career cluster sheets will be used in conjunction with other activities in this book.

Flexibility

The activities vary in length of time required for completion. Some can be completed in as short a period as 15 minutes, and others require more time. A good mix of short, middle-range, and long-term projects are provided. The activities can be used in class or assigned as homework or extra credit projects. Many of these activities require skills in reading, language arts, social studies, math, and study skills. This simplifies integrating the activities into academic subject areas if you choose.

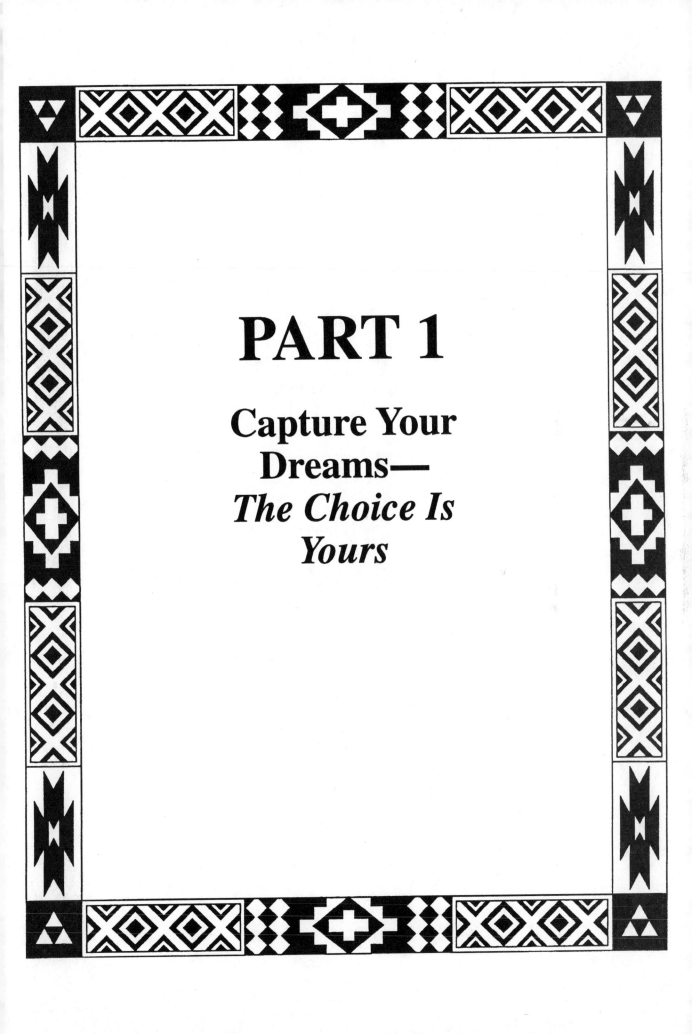

PART 1

Capture Your Dreams—
The Choice Is Yours

Activity Sheet #1
Code: I

Write a Letter Home

Do the adults in your house ever ask you, "What did you do in school today?" Sometimes that's hard to answer! This activity will help you share information about what you'll be doing with your new *Dream Catchers* book.

> ***INSTRUCTIONS:*** Write a letter to your parent(s) or guardian(s) about your new *Dream Catchers* book. Your teacher will explain the correct form for setting up your letter, or you can look up letter writing rules in your language book. If you decide to mail the letter, make sure you address the envelope correctly too.

Paragraph 1—Give the title and the subtitle of your book. (Check your language book for the correct way to write book titles.) Explain that this is a new book you are just starting to use.

Paragraph 2—Copy the following information for your letter.

"*Dream Catchers* is a three-part book that will help me learn about the world of work. In Part 1, I will learn about different career choices and the skills needed to understand and use career information. In Part 2, I will learn how schoolwork and jobs are connected. I will study skills needed for both schoolwork and jobs. I will also learn about all the different places to get education or training for jobs. In Part 3, I will learn how ability, effort, and achievement will help me be successful in school and when I get a job. This will give me lots of ways to improve my study skills and work habits."

Paragraph 3—Explain that you will need your parent(s), guardian(s), or other adults to help you learn about working. You will be interviewing them about the different kinds of work they do—jobs, volunteer work, or housework.

Paragraph 4—(OPTIONAL) You might want to explain the Indian legend about Dream Catchers which is in the front of your book. You might even want to draw a Dream Catcher on the back of your letter.

■ *EXTRA ACTIVITY*—Letter Exchange

Exchange letters with a classmate. Proofread one another's letter. Make sure they are written in the correct form, punctuated correctly, and do not contain spelling errors. Write a final, corrected copy of your letter if needed.

Activity Sheet #2
Code: I, 2 Pages

Make Your Own Dream Catcher

This activity will teach you how to make your own Dream Catcher. To make it easier to see what you will be doing, look at the picture of a Dream Catcher in your activity book.

INSTRUCTIONS: Follow the steps below to construct your Dream Catcher. Don't worry if your frame isn't perfectly round. You may add other decorations if you wish—this is your own creation!

Materials Needed

- Bendable materials to make the Dream Catcher frame. You can use grapevines or any branches or twigs that are soft enough to bend into a circle without cracking.

NOTE: Many craft or garden stores sell grapevine wreaths that can be taken apart to make several frames.

- Waxed string. (Available in craft or leather stores.)
- A large feather. It should be at least 6 inches long. (Use either a real one or make one from construction paper and pipe cleaners.)
- Beads or other decorations. (One bead should have a center hole about 3/8 inch in diameter.)

STEP 1: Making the Frame

1. Cut one piece of waxed string about 6 inches long.
2. Take one long (16 to 20 inches) grapevine and make a mark in the middle of it.
3. Shape the grapevine into a circle taking one end and bending it to the middle mark.
4. Take the remaining "straight" part of your grapevine. Twist it around the circle you just made by going over and under the circle.
5. Tie the circle together with the waxed string where the ends meet. If you have any "loose" spots in your frame, you can tie those with waxed string too.

STEP 2: Making the Web

1. Cut six pieces of waxed string that are at least 6 inches longer than the width of your frame.
2. Take one piece of string and tie it to the top of your frame. Tie the other end to the bottom, making the string as tight as you can.
3. Take another piece of string, repeat the step above going from side to side on your Dream Catcher frame. You now have your frame circle divided into four sections,

like pie slices. You are going to continue to divide those four sections into smaller sections.

4. Make two marks in each of the four sections on the frame to divide each section into thirds. (You will make a total of eight marks on your frame.)
5. Tie a piece of string to a mark in one section. Tie the end of the same string to the mark on the exact opposite side of the frame. This will give you two more "pie" pieces. Continue with the remaining pieces of string. When you are done, your frame will be divided into 12 sections.
6. To finish your web, cut a piece of string about 15 inches long. Tie that string as tightly as you can to any string on your frame, making sure it's about 3/4 inch away from the frame.
7. Take the string and begin weaving it around all the strings in your web to form a circle inside your frame (like a spider web).

NOTE: To secure the string in place, weave it under a string tied to your frame. Pass the string you are holding around and under again to form a "loop" around the string tied to the frame. Pull your loop so it is tight.

Make another "loop" on the next string tied to the frame. Keep repeating this process until you have made a complete circle. Tie a knot with the string when you finish the circle and cut off any extra string.

8. Make as many "inner circles" as you want following the directions above to finish your web.

STEP 3: Adding the Feather

1. Take the feather and slip a bead with a 3/4 inch hole through the "quill" end of it—pushing the bead down about 2 inches. (If you make your own feather, use a pipe cleaner for the quill end.)
2. Put the feather in the center of your Dream Catcher web where all the strings cross or any other place you wish. Bend the quill so it is on the other side of the crossed strings.
3. Push the bead up on your feather so it covers the bent quill end to hold your feather to the web.

STEP 4: Finishing Your Dream Catcher

1. Using another piece of waxed string, tie a loop to the top of your Dream Catcher for hanging.
2. You can cut off any extra string hanging from your Dream Catcher frame or you can tie beads on the ends of the strings for decoration.

Activity Sheet #3
Code: I, SG, 2 Pages

Make Your Own Cluster Games

In your *Dream Catchers* book, you learned about "clusters." A cluster is a group of things that are put together because they are alike in some ways. You can have fun with clusters! This activity will show you three different games you can make and play with clusters. Other ideas for cluster games are on the back of this sheet.

> ***INSTRUCTIONS:*** Follow the steps below to play each of the cluster games.

Name That Cluster!

1. Make two columns on a sheet of notebook paper. Label the left-hand column "Things in the Cluster" Label the right-hand column "Cluster Name."
2. List the names of things that can be grouped together under the "Things in the Cluster" column. (Try to think of several different groups.) Leave the "Cluster Name" column blank. For example:

THINGS IN THE CLUSTER						CLUSTER NAME
1.	Apple	Orange	Banana	Grape	Pear	

3. Give your paper to a classmate and have them try to guess the cluster names.

Cluster Cards

1. Write four different cluster names on a sheet of paper. List five things that would fit into each cluster and don't let anyone see your paper.
2. Make 20 cards from index cards or notebook paper.

> ***NOTE:*** Fold the long sides of notebook paper in half. Then fold the paper in half from top to bottom and you will have four rectangles. Tear along the fold lines to make your cards. Repeat the process to get 20 cards.

3. Write one name of each thing in your clusters on each card. When you are done, each card should have a different name on it.
4. Mix up all your cards. Give them to a classmate. Have your classmate arrange the cards into four clusters and try to guess each of your cluster names.

Cluster Art

1. Look through old magazines and newspapers and find pictures of things you could put into clusters. (For example: athletes, breakfast foods, cars, etc.) Make as many clusters as you want.
2. Paste your pictures on cardboard or paper to keep them from tearing.
3. Mix up all your pages and give them to a classmate. Have your classmate arrange the pictures into clusters and give each cluster a name.

More Cluster Games

Clusters can be made from many things. You can also use cluster games to help study and review your schoolwork and have fun at the same time! You can make clusters from all the subjects you are studying in school. Use your textbooks to help. Some examples are given below:

1. **Language**—Make clusters of nouns, verbs, adjectives, adverbs, or book titles, or quotations.
2. **Math**—Number clusters can be great fun and offer lots of good "brainteaser" possibilities for trying to find a name for the cluster. For instance, you can use numbers that can be divided by 6, or numbers that end in 2, or even numbers, or fractions. Try to stump your classmates.
3. **Spelling**—Make clusters of words that have silent e's or double vowels or compound words.
4. **Social Studies**—Make clusters of mountain ranges, or countries in Europe, or names of lakes, or state capitols.
5. **Science**—Make clusters of flowering plants, or mammals, or types of weather, or natural resources.

Activity Sheet #4
Code: SG

Career Cluster Collages

A collage is a way to make a piece of art by arranging different materials together and pasting them on a hard surface. Making collages is a good way to have fun and learn at the same time.

INSTRUCTIONS: Follow the steps below to create career collages. When you are finished, decorate a bulleting board in your classroom or hang your collages on the wall outside your classroom door for the whole school to see. (Be sure to get your teacher's permission first.)

1. You will need to divide into nine small groups. Each group will be assigned a different career cluster.
2. Each group should get a "Career Cluster Worksheet" from your teacher.
3. As a group, list as many jobs as you can think of that belong in your cluster on the "Career Cluster Worksheet." You can use the jobs listed in your *Dream Catchers* book to get you started. Add any others you can think of.
4. Each group member should look through magazines and newspapers at home and bring in several pictures of people working at jobs in your cluster. You can also draw or trace pictures.
5. Get a poster board or a piece of cardboard to paste your pictures on.
6. Layout your collage. Trim your pictures into different shapes. When you make a collage, many of the pictures overlap, and you don't want any poster board to show. Experiment with different layouts. Put your "Career Cluster Worksheet" and your pictures on your poster board until you find an arrangement you all like.
7. Paste your "Career Cluster Worksheet" and pictures to your poster board.

Activity Sheet #5
Code: I, SG

Agriculture and Natural Resource Cluster Worksheet

Agriculture and Natural Resources Cluster

In this cluster, people breed, grow, care for, and gather plants and animals and their products. They also catch, hunt, and trap animal life. They may do work like: 1) grow crops; 2) raise cattle or other animals; 3) grow, care for, and harvest forests; 4) grow plants in a greenhouse, and 5) catch fish.

Activity Sheet #6
Code: I, SG

Business and Marketing Cluster Worksheet

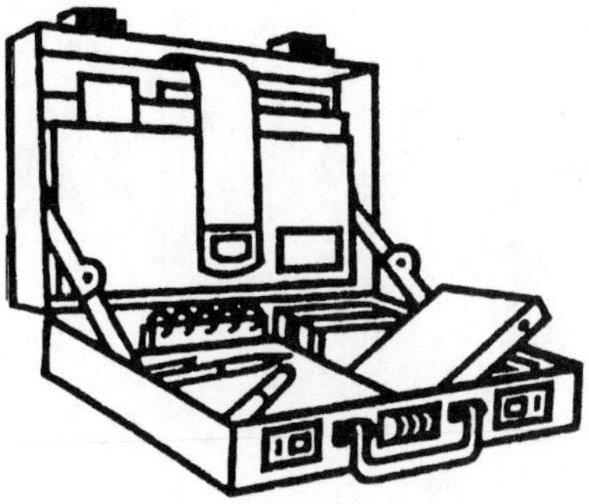

Business and Marketing Cluster

In this cluster, people have jobs that keep businesses running every day. They may do work like: 1) make plans; 2) give directions to other people; 3) sell things; 4) talk to customers; 5) type letters and reports; 6) work on a computer or other business machines, and 7) keep track of money.

Activity Sheet #7
Code: I, SG

Communication, Art, and Design Cluster Worksheet

Communication, Art and Design Cluster

In this cluster, people create things to express ideas, thoughts or feelings. They may do work like: 1) draw pictures by hand or on a computer; 2) write stories or newspaper articles; 3) take photographs; 4) act in a play or movie; 5) play music or sing; 6) arrange flowers, and 7) talk on TV or radio.

Activity Sheet #8
Code: I, SG

Construction and Production Cluster Worksheet

Construction and Production Cluster

In this cluster, people build, fix, and make things. *Construction* workers may do work like: 1) build a house, building, bridge, or road; 2) put in plumbing; 3) fix a road, and 4) operate a bulldozer. *Production* workers may do work like: 1) put together a car; 2) take coal out of mines; 3) make tools, and 4) build furniture.

Activity Sheet #9
Code: I, SG

Education, Human Services, and Personal Service Cluster Worksheet

Education, Human Services, and Personal Service Cluster

In this cluster, people teach or help other people. *Education* workers may do work like: 1) teach children or adults, and 2) help people find books in a library. *Human services* workers may do work like: 1) listen to people's problems and try to help solve them, and 2) help people understand the law. *Personal service* workers may do work like:
1) cut or style hair; 2) take care of lawns; 3) prepare food; 4) guard or protect people or things, and 5) fight fires.

Activity Sheet #10
Code: I, SG

Health Cluster Worksheet

Health Cluster

In this cluster, people try to prevent illness. They also take care of people or animals who are sick. They may do work like: 1) take care of sick people in a hospital or at home; 2) give shots; 3) make medicine; 4) fix teeth; 5) run tests in a lab; 6) take X-Rays, and 7) give eye and hearing tests.

Health Officer Worksheet

Activity Sheet #11
Code: I, SG

Repairers and Mechanics Cluster Worksheet

Repairers and Mechanics Cluster

In this cluster, people fix and take care of all kinds of big and small machines. They may do work like: 1) repair dents in cars and trucks; 2) check airplane engines; 3) fix broken TV's or VCR's; 4) repair robots or computers; 5) put in electric power lines; 6) fix machines in a factory, and 7) repair watches.

Activity Sheet #12
Code: I, SG

Science and Technology Cluster Worksheet

Science and Technology Cluster

In this cluster, people do scientific research to discover, collect, and analyze knowledge. They use this knowledge to solve problems or invent new things. They may do work like: 1) try to find a cure for a disease; 2) test food for safety; 3) improve airplane designs; 4) discover ways to stop pollution; 5) invent new products or things, and 6) predict earthquakes.

Activity Sheet #13
Code: I, SG

Transportation Cluster Worksheet

Transportation Cluster

In this cluster, people help move people or things from one place to another. They may do work like: 1) drive a taxi, bus, truck, or train; 2) fly an airplane; 3) help passengers on an airplane, ship, or train; 4) guide planes from the ground; 5) move boxes and large objects, and 6) load or take things off a ship.

Activity Sheet #14
Code: I, SG

You Work with People and Animals Too!

In your *Dream Catchers* book, you learned that jobs can be put into groups by who or what people do most of their work with. One of these groups was "People and Animals."

In this group, people spend most of their time working with other people or animals. Their jobs involve helping or serving people or animals. For example: a nurse, a teacher, a taxi driver, a salesperson, a zoo keeper and a veterinarian all have jobs where they work with people or animals.

INSTRUCTIONS: Think of all the activities you do with other people or animals. Write them on the lines below.

■ *EXTRA ACTIVITY*—Make a Class List of People and Animal Activities

1. Work in a small group. Collect everyone's worksheet on people and animal activities. Divide them among group members.
2. Read out loud the worksheet with the longest list. Have group members cross out an activity if it's on their worksheet. Compare what's left on all worksheets and cross out duplicates.
3. Get a marker and a big sheet of paper. Use "People and Animal Activities" for your title and write your group's list on the paper. Hang your list somewhere in the classroom.

Activity Sheet #15
Code: I, SG

You Work with Things and Machinery Too!

In your *Dream Catchers* book, you learned that jobs can be put into groups by who or what people do most of their work with. One of these groups was "Things and Machinery."

In this group, people work every day with things or machinery. Their jobs involve working with things that are not alive. For example: a carpenter, a factory worker, an automobile repair person, a laboratory scientist, and a computer operator all have jobs where they work with things or machinery.

> ***INSTRUCTIONS:*** Think of all the activities you do with things and machinery. Write them on the lines below.

____

____

____

____

____

____

____

____

____

____

■ *EXTRA ACTIVITY*—Make a Class List of Things and Machinery Activities

1. Work in a small group. Collect everyone's worksheet on things and machinery activities. Divide them among group members.
2. Read out loud the worksheet with the longest list. Have group members cross out an activity if it's on their worksheet. Compare what's left on all worksheets and cross out duplicates.
3. Get a marker and a big sheet of paper. Use "Things and Machinery Activities" for your title and write your group's list on the paper. Hang your list somewhere in the classroom.

Activity Sheet #16
Code: I, SG

You Work with Data Too!

In your *Dream Catchers* book, you learned that jobs can be put into groups by who or what people do most of their work with. One of these groups was "Data."

In this group, people work everyday with information and facts. They may explain, collect, organize or study information. For example: a newspaper editor, a police artist, a chemist, a weather person, and a safety inspector all have jobs where they work with information and facts.

Some people work gathering information and facts that they use in new or creative ways. We describe this activity as having ideas. For example: a writer, an artist, an inventor, and a designer all have jobs where they use data in creative or new ways.

INSTRUCTIONS: Think of all the activities you do using data. Write them on the lines below.

____

____

____

____

____

____

____

____

____

____

■ *EXTRA ACTIVITY*—Make a Class List of Data Activities

1. Work in a small group. Collect everyone's worksheet on data activities. Divide them among group members.
2. Read out loud the worksheet with the longest list. Have group members cross out an activity if it's on their worksheet. Compare what's left on all worksheets and cross out duplicates.
3. Get a marker and a big sheet of paper. Use "Data Activities" for your title and write your group's list on the paper. Hang your list somewhere in the classroom.

Activity Sheet #17
Code: I, SG, 2 Pages

Discovering More Working Conditions

In your *Dream Catchers* book, you learned that jobs could be grouped together by their working conditions. You did an activity on the working conditions "Inside" or "Outside." But there are more.

INSTRUCTIONS: The list below contains other kinds of working conditions. After each one, make a list of as many jobs as you can think of in the spaces provided. (Name either the job title or describe the job.)

Both Inside and Out

Workers spend about half their time inside buildings or things that protect them from weather and half their time outside.

____

____

____

____

Noise Level

Workers are exposed to noise levels so high that the noise can distract them or cause hearing loss.

____

____

____

____

Temperature

Workers are exposed to temperatures of heat or cold that are so extreme that the body will react to them.

____

____

____

____

Safety

Workers perform their jobs under conditions that can cause danger to life, health, or risk of bodily injury.

____

____

____

____

■ *EXTRA ACTIVITY*

You can do this activity in small groups and compete with one another. The group that has the most jobs for all categories wins.

Activity Sheet #18
Code: C

Conduct a Work Force Survey

In your *Dream Catchers* book, you learned that workers can be divided into two groups by who they work for. "Employees" are workers who work for others. "Self-employed" means that you own your own business and work for yourself.

Although most people work as employees, the number of self-employed people in the work force is growing every year. As a class, do a work force survey to discover how many people you know who are employees or self-employed. (A survey is when you gather information and analyze the results.)

INSTRUCTIONS: Follow the steps below to conduct your own survey and compile the results. Each person in the class must gather the data.

1. Ask at least five adults you know if they are an employee or self-employed. (You can record their answers on the back of this paper.) Also ask them their job title.
2. Bring your research to class.
3. Add up the total number of employees and self-employed people from all data gathered.
4. Figure out the percentage of employees and self-employed people from your survey. If you haven't done percentages yet in math, your teacher can do it for you or show you how.
5. Make a list of the kinds of jobs self-employed people have from the data you gathered. Do they do the same kind of work as people who are employees? How many different kinds of self-employed jobs did your survey reveal?

■ *EXTRA ACTIVITY*—Interview a Self-Employed Person

If you found someone who was self-employed when gathering data, interview them and write a report to share with your class. Some questions you might ask are:

- What kind of work do you do?
- How did you decide to work for yourself?
- Did you work for someone else before you started your own business? What did you do?
- What do you like about being self-employed?
- What do you dislike about being self-employed?

Activity Sheet #19
Code: I

Career Data Worksheet

Name: ______________________________

Date: ______________________________

Source of Information: ______________________________

Job Title: ______________________________

What Career Cluster does this job belong in? ______________________________

____

Is the work mostly with People and Animals, Things and Machinery, or Data? __________

____

What are the Working Conditions? Describe the workplace. ______________________________

____

____

Would you likely be an employee or self-employed? ______________________________

____

Describe the kind of work done on this job. ______________________________

____

____

Describe the skills needed for this job. ______________________________

____

____

Where can the skills for this job be learned? ______________________________

____

____

Can either a woman or man do this job? (Yes or No). Explain your answer. __________

____

____

____

____

Activity Sheet #20
Code: I

Write a Letter Requesting Career Information

Many organizations offer free brochures that give information on specific occupations. Write a letter of inquiry ("inquiry" means to ask for something) for information on a career that interests you. Your teacher can help you find the addresses of places to write. Follow the instructions below.

INSTRUCTIONS: A letter of inquiry has six parts: heading, inside address, greeting, body, closing, and signature. Write your letter following the steps below.

1. **Heading**—Write your address and the date on the top right-hand side of your paper. Skip two lines.
2. **Inside Address**—Write "Career Information Director" and the address you are writing to at the left-hand margin. Skip a line.
3. **Greeting**—Write "Dear Career Information Director:"
4. **Body**

   Introduction—Give your name, grade, and school. Tell the person you are studying about careers in your class.

   Body—Write a paragraph requesting any free brochures or information on the career you select. Make sure to name the career. Tell the person why you want the information.

   Closing—Write a paragraph thanking the person for sending you the information. Tell them you are looking forward to receiving it.
5. **Closing**—Write "Sincerely yours,"
6. **Signature**—Write your first and last name.
7. **Envelope**—Write your full name and address (including the zip code) in the upper left-hand corner. Address the envelope to "Career Information Director" and use the full inside address in the letter. Check your language book for examples if you need to.

Activity Sheet #21
Code: I

Careers of Famous People

A biography or autobiography is the story of a person's life.

Sometimes people are famous because of the work they did. Have your school librarian or teacher help you find a biography or autobiography that tells about someone's life and work.

INSTRUCTIONS: Read the biography or autobiography. Write a book report answering the questions below. If your book doesn't give you information on some of the questions, just skip them.

1 What is the book title, who is the author, and how many pages is the book?
2. What kind of work did this person do that made him or her famous? Describe some of this person's accomplishments.
3. How did the person get interested in this kind of work?
4. Did the person have to have any special training or education to learn their work? How did he or she learn the skills needed for the job?
5. Did the person have to try very hard to accomplish his or her goals? What did they do? How long did it take?
6. Did this person have any failures before he or she succeeded? What happened?
7. What part of this book did you like the most? Why?
8. Would you like to do this kind of work? Explain why or why not.

Activity Sheet #22
Code: C

Make a Career Cluster Handbook

When your class has finished doing career research using the "Career Data Worksheets," make a handbook with all the worksheets. Keep this book in your classroom library for study purposes.

INSTRUCTIONS: Follow the steps below to assemble and bind your class handbook on careers.

1. Divide the worksheets into career cluster groups. Each separate cluster will be a chapter in your book.
2. Divide the class into small groups. Assign each group one cluster to work with.
3. Get another "Career Cluster Worksheet" that matches your cluster from your teacher.
4. Alphabetize the "Career Data Worksheets" in your cluster by the job title.
5. List the job titles in your cluster on the "Career Cluster Worksheet" in alphabetical order. This activity sheet will be the Table of Contents for your cluster.
6. Proofread to correct any errors in all your "Career Data Worksheets." (You may need to re-copy some of the worksheets.)

OPTIONAL: You may want to draw illustrations for the jobs in your cluster or bring in pictures from magazines. If you use magazine pictures, paste them to a piece of notebook paper.

7. Organize your chapter. Put the "Career Cluster Worksheet" first and then the "Career Data Worksheets" following in alphabetical order.
8. Select someone, or a group, to draw a cover for the handbook on an 8-1/2" x 11" sheet of paper. Insert or paste the cover on a 3-ring binder notebook.
9. Three-hole punch all the pages and put them in the notebook in the correct alphabetical order.
10. Select someone to make a Table of Contents for the whole handbook listing all the clusters in alphabetical order.

■ *EXTRA ACTIVITY*—Career Cluster Research

If you have clusters with no jobs or only a few jobs in them, class members might volunteer to do more career research in that cluster. If you learn about more careers during the year, add them to the class handbook. Perhaps you might want to donate your handbook to the library when the school year is over.

Activity Sheet #23
Code: I, C

Plan a Job Fair

A "job fair" is when people who work at different jobs gather together to explain their work to an audience. You've already done some research on jobs using your "Career Data Worksheet." This means you could explain this work to an audience also.

> ***INSTRUCTIONS:*** You and your classmates can use the information on the worksheets to present your own job fair. Follow the instructions below to help you plan.

1. Select the careers you want to present from your "Career Data Worksheets."
2. Using the information from the worksheet, decide what you will tell the audience. (You should know the information well enough so you don't have to read it.)
3. If the job requires any special tools that you can bring to class, plan to bring the tools with you on the day of the presentation.
4. Dress the part! On the day you give your presentation, wear the clothes a person would normally wear for that job.
5. Remember to ask for questions from the audience after you give your presentation.

■ *EXTRA ACTIVITY*—Job Fair for All

Your class might like to invite another class to attend your job fair.

Activity Sheet #24
Code: I, SG

Write a Wild Work Story!

Did you know that in the United States, there are over 12,000 different job titles? That's a lot of jobs! You know about many different kinds of jobs. But this activity will introduce you to many jobs you probably never heard about.

INSTRUCTIONS: Listed below are titles and descriptions of some jobs. Write a story on a separate sheet of paper using as many of the jobs as you can. You'll have to let your imagination run wild to get all these different kinds of jobs in one story.

1. **Custom Bow Maker**—selects, laminates, shapes and finishes wood, plastic and metal to make archery bows.
2. **Make-Up Artist**—applies make-up to performers to change their appearance to fit the parts they are playing.
3. **Seismologist**—studies and interprets information to locate earthquakes and earthquake faults.
4. **Siviculturist**—plants new trees and takes care of forests to make sure the trees grow well.
5. **Horse Exerciser**—rides racehorses to exercise and condition them for horse racing.
6. **Airline Security Representative**—checks passengers for weapons, explosives or other forbidden things to prevent people from taking them into the airport or on an airplane.
7. **Rocket Engine Component Mechanic**—puts together and tests the mechanical parts of rocket engines.
8. **Chef de Froid**—designs and prepares decorated foods and artistically arranges foods for buffets in fancy restaurants.
9. **Laser-Beam Machine Operator**—operates a laser-beam machine which produces heat from a light beam to weld metal parts together.
10. **Telecommunicator**—operates communication equipment. Sends people and equipment to the scene of an emergency.
11. **Cryptographic Machine Operator**—operates cryptographic machines to code, transmit, and decode secret messages for the military, police departments, or businesses.

Activity Sheet #25
Code: I

Pick Your "Dream" Career

It's always fun to dream so let's do it. If you could be whatever you wanted to be for one day, what would you choose? A movie star? A professional sports figure? President of the United States? A rock singer? An astronaut? A surgeon? For this activity you can be whatever you want to be, then write about it following the instructions below.

INSTRUCTIONS: Write a story on the lines below about what you did for one day in the career you select. Be sure to write the name of your career on the blank line, in the title, and in the first sentence.

One Day in the Life of a ______________________________

I am a ______________________________

This is what I did today: ______________________________

Activity Sheet #26
Code: C, 2 Pages

What's My Line?

Several years ago, there was a quiz show on television called "What's My Line?" A contestant would come on the show and a group of four people, called the panel, would ask the contestant questions to try and guess his or her job. The panel could only ask questions that could be answered "Yes" or "No." They had to guess the job in 20 questions or the contestant won.

INSTRUCTIONS: Your class can have a lot of fun playing "What's My Line" following the rules below. Assign members of your class the following roles:

- 1 game show host or hostess
- 1 guest contestant
- 4 panel members

NOTE: The rest of the class will be the audience. They should sit back and enjoy the show!

Materials Needed

- A piece of paper or cardboard on which to write the guest's occupation.
- 20 index cards, pieces of paper, or cardboard. Number them from 1 to 20. (Each card gets one number.)

Arrange the "set." Put two desks in the front of the room for the host and guest. Put four desks together, next to or across from the other two, for the panel. Make sure to arrange the desks so the audience can see everyone.

Game Rules

1. The host brings out the panel and introduces them to the audience.
2. The host then brings out the guest and introduces him or her. Everyone should be seated at their desks.
3. The host shows the audience the card with the guest's occupation written on it without letting the panel see. (On the TV show, the panel wore blindfolds for the whole game!)

OPTIONAL RULE: Do not show the guest's occupation to the audience. If the panel fails to guess the correct occupation after 20 questions, the moderator may call on five people in the audience, and they can try to guess the occupation.

4. The panel asks questions to try and guess the occupation. Panel members can only ask a question that can be answered "Yes" or "No." If they ask a question that can't be answered "Yes" or "No," the host must tell them it's an illegal question, and to rephrase it. Panel members take turns asking questions until the 20 questions are used up.
5. The host has the 20 number cards on his or her desk with number 20 on the top. The cards should be displayed or held so the audience and panel can see them. Each time a panel member asks a question, the host removes one card. This way, everyone knows how many questions are left.
6. After 20 questions, each panel member has one chance to guess the occupation. For example, one may ask, "Are you a fireman?" If no one guesses correctly, the guest wins the game.

Hints for Asking Good Questions

Make sure to use your new knowledge about careers to try and guess the occupation. You can ask the guest if he or she works with People and Animals, Things and Machinery, or Data. You can ask the career cluster, the working conditions, if the job requires special education or training, etc. The guest should probably check with your teacher before the game starts to make sure he or she knows the correct career cluster.

Activity Sheet #27
Code: I, SG

Work in Early America

In social studies, you learned how people in America lived in the past. Think of the time when America was a new nation just being settled. People lived very differently in those times then we do now.

When times change, the kinds of work people do also changes. For example, one job that no longer exists from earlier times is wagon making. The way work is done also changes. For example, most women used to hand-sew all the clothes for their families. Now clothes are made on sewing machines, often in factories, and people buy their clothes in stores. This activity will help you see how work is done different now.

INSTRUCTIONS: Use your social studies book and library books to learn about America's early settlers. Each person in class might read a book about America's early days. Then follow the instructions below. You can do this activity by yourself or in small groups.

1. Make separate lists on large paper for the categories that follow. You may want to divide the subjects into smaller groups.
   - Early American Jobs That Are Now Gone
   - Early American Work Done by One or Few People Now Done by Businesses or in Factories
   - Things We Buy that the Early Settlers Made for Themselves
   - Household Work and Chores Early Settlers Did That No Longer Exist
2. Write the information under the categories using markers. Draw on the paper to illustrate certain jobs if you want to. You can display your lists in the classroom.

Activity Sheet #28
Code: I, SG, C

Inventions Create Jobs!

When someone invents something new that people need, the invention can create new jobs. You might need people to make it, use it, repair it, sell it, etc. Just think of all the jobs created by Thomas Edison's inventions with electricity. This activity will help you learn about how new jobs are created.

INSTRUCTIONS: Use your social studies book to research early inventions like the telegraph, light bulb, and steam engine. You will also want to know about inventions like the telephone, television, VCR's, and airplanes.

1. Make a list of all the inventions you can think of that have changed the way people live. Use your social studies book if you need help.
2. When your list is done, choose some of your inventions and make a list of all the jobs you can think of that were created because of this invention. Give your list a title, for example, "Jobs Created by the Invention of the Airplane" and list all the jobs under the title.
3. You may want to do this activity in small groups. As a class, make a list of inventions. Then divide the list among several small groups. Have each group make lists of jobs created by their inventions.

Activity Sheet #29
Code: I, SG, C

Jobs of the Future

You have learned that inventions create new jobs. People are always inventing new things. That means new jobs will keep being created! This is good news for you if you plan to enter the work force some day.

INSTRUCTIONS: Let's take a trip to the year 3000. Pretend we are now in the thirtieth century. Follow the steps below to see what life and work will be like in the future.

1. Make a list of things that have been invented that change the way people live and work.
2. When your list is done, choose some of your inventions and make a list of all the jobs you can think of that were created because of this invention. Give your list a title, for example, "Jobs Created by the Invention of the Wangdoodle." Explain what the Wangdoodle is or does. Then list all the jobs created by this invention.
3. You may want to do this activity in small groups. As a group, make a list of inventions. Then think of jobs created by the inventions.

OPTIONAL: You may want to draw some pictures of your inventions and tell what they do.

Activity Sheet #30
Code: I

Job Genealogy

Genealogy is the study of ancestry or family histories. (We often call this "building a family tree.") Another way to see how jobs change is to study the kinds of jobs people in a family have worked at.

INSTRUCTIONS: To build a job family tree, follow these instructions. You must first select a family to research. You can use your own family, or a relatives' or neighbors' family. You will conduct your research by interviewing.

1. Decide which side of the family you will research. (You can research both sides of the family, mother and father, or do only one side.)
2. Go back as far in the family history as the people you are interviewing can remember. For example, great-grandparents, great-great grandparents, etc.
3. Ask the person you are interviewing the following questions. (Start with the oldest family member this person can remember and work down to your generation.)
   - Name of the family member.
   - Name of the job(s) they had. (Many people work more than one job in a lifetime. Make sure to include all the jobs that person had as an adult. Also, make sure to include homemaking as a job. If they can't remember certain people's jobs, put "unknown" on the family tree.)
4. Your teacher will show you how to draw a genealogical chart (family tree). Draw a genealogical chart using the data you gathered in your research.

Activity Sheet #31
Code: I

Workplaces in Your Community

Many workplaces in your community need lots of different kinds of workers to keep the business operating. Think about all the different places you've been where people work: a supermarket, department store, hospital, library, restaurant, or gas station. Do people in those workplaces have different jobs?

INSTRUCTIONS: This activity will help you explore different workplaces in your community and the different jobs people do in the same workplace. Follow the steps below to learn more about where people work.

1. Draw a big picture of any workplace in your community you chose.
2. Describe all the different kinds of jobs people do in that workplace. Write them on a piece of paper.
3. Staple or glue your paper to your picture.
4. Display your picture somewhere in your classroom. Maybe your teacher will let you do a "Workplaces in Our Community" bulletin board.

Activity Sheet #32
Code: I, C

Volunteer Work in Your Community

In your *Dream Catchers* book, you learned that many people do work for free. This is called volunteer work. Find an adult or older brother or sister who has done volunteer work. Interview them to learn about what they did.

> *INSTRUCTIONS:* Sample questions you can ask for your interview are listed below. You can add any other questions you want during the interview. Make sure to carefully write down the person's name and answers on a separate sheet of paper.

1. What kind of volunteer work have you done? Describe as many volunteer activities as possible.
2. How did you find out about doing volunteer work?
3. Did you need any special training to do your volunteer work? If so, how did you get the training?
4. Why do you do volunteer work?
5. Do you think it's everyone's responsibility to volunteer some of their time? Why?

■ *EXTRA ACTIVITY*—Report on Volunteer Work

1. Share your research with your classmates. Write a report from the information you gathered during your interview. You might read your report out loud or your teacher may have the class do a "volunteer work" bulletin board.
2. Compare everyone's research results. Make a big list to hang in the classroom of all the different kinds of volunteer work the class learned about.
3. Investigate volunteer activities for younger people in your community. Many communities have special volunteer organizations for young people. They work in hospitals, for Teen Hotlines, at their place of worship, etc. Have your teacher help you learn about volunteer activities for younger people. The phone book might be a good place to start researching.

Activity Sheet #33
Code: C, 2 Pages

Plan a Class Volunteer Project

People often do volunteer work to help others or to improve the environment in their community. As a class, plan a project where you can help others or improve the environment.

You can select a simple project like cleaning up your school yard or serving as helpers in the younger grades in your school. You can also select a more complex project where you earn money and donate it to a charity or buy something your school needs. The instructions below are for a more complex project because that takes more time and planning. If you select a simple project, your teacher can help you plan it.

> ***INSTRUCTIONS:*** Decide what your class money-making project will be. You can have a garage sale where the class brings in toys, books, and other items the children in your school would like to buy. You may decide to make something to sell like popcorn and lemonade. Or you might decide to bake something simple to sell during lunch. Decide how you will use the money you earn.

Planning Your Project

Decide what tasks are involved:

- How will you gather the items to sell if you have a garage sale?
- If you are making something to eat or drink, what quantities will you make? (For example, how many bags of popcorn will you need?)
- What ingredients will you need to make your product? What materials will you need to package your product? (For example, if you sell popcorn, will you put it in bags? Do you need to buy cups for refreshments?)
- If you need to buy supplies, how much will you buy? How much will it cost? (These costs are your "expenses.") Who will buy the materials you need? Where will you get the money? (You may need to take out a business loan.)
- Will you have any other expenses? For example, if you are going to bake something, how much will the ingredients cost?
- Figure out your estimated profit. Subtract your expenses from how much money you think you will make.
- How will you advertise your project? How often? Do you need to prepare a handout for classmates to take home?
- Do you need to get permission from your principal or ask other teachers if they will bring their classes to your sale? How will you do that?
- If you are going to use your classroom for the sale, how will you need to arrange the desks and chairs? Do you need to make any signs to use in the room? How will you organize the items if you have a garage sale?
- If you are going to make something, where and when will you make it? What day will you have your sale?

Make a Schedule and Assign Planning Tasks

1. On a calendar or a sheet of paper, assign days and deadlines for all the tasks you listed and any others you may have added.
2. Decide which tasks will be done in school and which tasks will be done at home or after class.
3. Assign workers who will perform the tasks and list them on the schedule. (Some tasks may be accomplished by small groups.) You may want to include a project manager who is responsible for making sure people complete their tasks on time. This is your volunteer project so your teacher should not be responsible for seeing that you do your tasks.

Day of the Sale Plan

1. Decide what tasks have to be performed on the day of the sale including set-up and preparation, the sale itself, and clean-up.
2. Decide what workers you will need on the sale day. For example, if you plan to prepare food that day, how many people do you need to prepare and package it? (Your teacher may explain what "mass production" is and help you organize assembly lines to produce your product.) You will need a cashier or two. You may need baggers. Assign workers.

After the Sale

1. Add up the money you took in. Subtract your expenses and pay your expense bills if you have any. What's left is your "profit."
2. Decide how you will donate your profit to the group you selected to give it to. For example, will you write a letter or present it in person? If you are going to buy something for your school, who will purchase it?

Activity Sheet #34
Code: I

Write a Letter Home—Part 1

You have now finished Part 1 of your *Dream Catchers* activity book. Write a letter home explaining what you have learned.

You can use your *Dream Catchers* book for help.

> *INSTRUCTIONS:* Write a letter home using the suggestions given below. Your teacher will explain the correct letter form, or you can look up rules for writing letters in your language book. If you decide to mail the letter, make sure you address the envelope correctly too.

Include the following information in your letter:

Paragraph 1—Give the title of your book and the section title for Part 1. (Check your language book for the correct way to write book titles and chapter titles.) Explain that you have just finished all the activities in Part 1.

Paragraph 2—Explain that you learned how jobs can be grouped together in many different ways. Explain what career clusters are and tell which cluster(s) interested you the most. (The ones you might like to work in someday.) You might even give the job titles of some of the jobs that you liked.

Paragraph 3—Explain that you learned jobs can also be grouped by who or what you work with (People and Animals, Things and Machinery, and Data and Ideas) and working conditions. Tell which of these groups interested you the most.

Paragraph 4—Tell what you learned about volunteer work and all the work it takes to run a home.

Paragraph 5—Explain which activity you liked the most in Part 1 and why.

■ *EXTRA ACTIVITY*—Letter Exchange

Exchange letters with a classmate. Proofread one another's letter. Make sure they are written in the correct form, are punctuated correctly, and do not contain spelling errors. Write a final, corrected copy of your letter if needed.

PART 2

The Stuff Dreams Are Made Of—
Discovering Your Skills

Activity Sheet #35
Code: I

Make a Skills Chain

In your *Dream Catchers* book, you learned that skills are like building blocks. One skill is made up of many other skills you have learned. Many times you must first be able to perform one skill in order to perform the next.

INSTRUCTIONS: This activity will help you analyze just one of your skills. It will also create a "guessing game" you can play with others.

Materials Needed

- scissors
- construction paper
- glue
- pen or black marker

1. Select a skill you have. (It can be anything from rowing a boat, to throwing a ball, to writing poetry, to painting your bedroom.) On a separate sheet of paper, write the skill. Underneath your skill, write all the other skills (we'll call these "sub-skills") you had to learn to be able to perform your skill. Put the sub-skills in the order that you had to learn them. (For example, you had to learn alphabet letters before you could learn the sounds each letter represents.)
2. Cut the construction paper in strips about 1 inch wide and 3 inches long. You will need one strip of paper for each sub-skill.
3. Write your sub-skills on the strips of paper, one sub-skill per strip. Your strips of paper will be glued into a circle to make a chain "link." Be sure to write your sub-skill large enough on the paper so it can be read after you make your link.
4. Make your skills chain. Glue your first skill strip in a circle to make your first link. Glue the next skill strip around the first link to begin making a chain. Continue this process until your chain is complete. Make sure to get your links in the right order. DO NOT include a link that names your skill.
5. Give your chain to a classmate to read. See if they can guess your skill. Trade your chain with several classmates.

■ *EXTRA ACTIVITY*—Link Your Skills

When you have finished your "guessing game," add a link to your chain that names your skill. Hang your chains to decorate your classroom. Or you can make one long chain from everyone's chain to show what a skilled class your are! Hang your long chain in your classroom.

Activity Sheet #36
Code: I

Make a Skills Bank

You probably have seen banks some people keep to save money. Maybe you even have a bank to help you save your allowance. A bank is a place set aside to store something valuable. It doesn't have to be money though.

> *INSTRUCTIONS:* This activity is about another kind of bank—a skills bank. It will help you to see all the skills you are learning. It will also show you how valuable your skills are. Follow the steps below.

Materials Needed

- a shoe box or a coffee can with lid
- scissors
- glue
- crayons or markers
- unlined paper

1. Cut a slot in the top of your shoe book or coffee can. You will need to make it large enough to insert folded pieces of paper.
2. Cut the unlined paper to fit the size of your bank in order to cover it. Use more than one piece if necessary.
3. Decorate the paper with crayons or markers. Make sure to write "My Skills Bank" and your name on the paper. Add any other decorations you want.
4. Glue the paper to your can or box.

How to Use Your Skills Bank

Pick a day once or twice a week when you will put skills in your bank. Write each skill on a piece of paper, fold it, and put it in your bank. You can put in any kind of skills you want that you've learned inside or outside of school. For example, when you finish a chapter in one of your books, you can write down a summary of what you've learned.

After several weeks have passed, open your skills bank and read all your skills. You may want to record them in a "New Skills Notebook." Then start saving your skills again.

Activity Sheet #37
Code: I, SG, C

Share Your Skills

In your *Dream Catchers* book, you learned that you have lots of skills. It's fun to share your skills with other people. This activity will suggest ways to share your skills with others.

INSTRUCTIONS: Select a skill you have (something you can make or do) that you can teach to other people. It can be anything simple or complicated. (If you are going to demonstrate your skill in the classroom to teach to other people, pick a skill you can do in class.)

1. Write instructions on how to perform your skill. To write clear instructions that people can understand. Follow the steps below:
   - Give your instructions a title that clearly and specifically states what the instructions are for. For example, "How to Make a Paper Airplane" or "How to Play Cat's Cradle" or "How to Jump Rope Double Dutch."
   - List all the tools or materials needed (if any) to follow the instructions. Put them under a heading "Tools and Materials Needed."
   - Give all instructions in step-by-step order, numbering each step. Each step should only give one instruction.
   - Each instruction should begin with a command word like "fold," "cut," "bend," "write," etc.
2. Draw illustrations if necessary to make your instructions clearer.

■ *EXTRA ACTIVITY*—Skills Demonstrations

1. Plan a "skills hour" once a week where classmates demonstrate their skills. You can pass out copies of your instructions to people who want them.
2. Exchange instructions with classmates. See if they can perform the skill following the instructions. (If they can't, the author may need to revise the instructions.)
3. Invite another class to your room for a "Skills Fair." Have several skills demonstrations take place in different areas in your classroom and let your visitors watch different demonstrations.

Activity Sheet #38
Code: I

You Can Be an Apprentice

One way people learn job-related skills is to be an apprentice. An apprentice works under a skilled worker who trains them how to do the job. The apprentice learns by doing the work with the guidance of the trainer.

> ***INSTRUCTIONS:*** You can be an apprentice by following the steps below. Bring this worksheet home so your trainer will understand what you need to do.

1. Have someone at home or in your neighborhood teach you how to do something new. It can be anything—how to cook something, iron a shirt, use a drill, change the oil in the car, or knit. Explain to your trainer that you want to learn a new skill, and they can help you select one.
2. Your trainer will show you how to perform the new skill. They may make you watch first before you can try it on your own. Or they may guide you through the steps as you try it the first time.
3. You have to keep practicing your new skill until you can do it correctly on your own without any help from your trainer. Then you have mastered the skill and are no longer an apprentice. Now you are a skilled worker.
4. Keep an "Apprentice Journal" of your learning process. Write down what you did each time you tried to learn your new skill. What mistakes did you make? What was hard? What was easy? What was fun? What was not fun? How long did it take to master your skill?
5. When you have mastered your skill, have your trainer sign and date your journal and state that you are now a skilled worker!

■ *EXTRA ACTIVITY*—What's Your Story?

You might want to share your experience with your classmates by turning your journal writings into a story. Draw illustrations too. Maybe you can do an "Apprentice Bulletin Board" with stories from the whole class.

Activity Sheet #39
Code: I

Practice Makes Perfect

You've probably heard the old saying, "Practice makes perfect." One of the reasons we have "old sayings" is because they are usually true! This activity will help you discover if that saying is true or not.

> ***INSTRUCTIONS:*** Pick a skill that you would like to improve or a new skill you would like to learn. It can be anything—an academic skill, an athletic skill, a musical skill, etc. Your teacher can suggest skills if you need help. Make it a skill that can be improved in one or two weeks.

1. Set up a goal sheet for yourself which includes the following information:
   - Describe your goal—what skill do you want to master?
   - Decide how much time per day, how many days per week, and how many weeks you will practice.
   - Describe what you are going to do when you practice.
2. Keep a practice journal. Write down what you did every day. How long did you actually practice? What did you do? Could you feel any improvement?
3. When the time is up (one or two weeks), answer these questions in your journal, "Does practice make perfect?" Did you really improve? Do you feel you've mastered your skill? Do you need more practice? If you didn't improve, why not?

■ *EXTRA ACTIVITY*—Share Your "Answers"

You can share your experience with other students in your class by reading your journal. See how other people answered the questions in step 3 above.

Activity Sheet #40
Code: I

What Academic Skills Are Needed for Jobs?

In your *Dream Catchers* book, you read some short stories that showed how people need academic skills for their jobs. Discover how important academic skills are!

> ***INSTRUCTIONS:*** In this activity, you will interview someone you know to learn more about how people use school subjects while they are working on the job. To conduct your interview follow the instructions below.

1. Select an adult you know to interview.
2. Ask them the following questions. Be sure to take good notes on what they say. You can use the back of this paper to write the answers. Remember, different jobs require different academic skills, so you will get some "No" answers.
   - What is your job?
   - Do you have to read on your job? What kinds of things do you read?
   - Do you have to communicate in writing on your job? What kinds of writing do you do?
   - Do you have to communicate by talking with others on your job? What kind of oral (talking) communication does your job require?
   - Do you use math on your job? How do you use it?
   - Do you have to use scientific information on your job? What do you use and how do you use it?
   - Do you have to use knowledge of social studies on your job? (This includes history, geography, government, information on other cultures or people, etc.) What information do you use?
   - Do you need to know a foreign language for your job? What language? How do you use it?
3. When you have finished your interview, use your notes to write a report called "Using Academic Skills at Work." Share your report with your classmates.

■ *EXTRA ACTIVITY*—List the Results

Instead of writing a report with your interview findings, combine the results of everyone's interviews into big lists you can display in your classroom. Make one list for each question asked. For example, make a list called "Reading at Work" and list all the different kinds of reading people need to do at work as discovered by all the interviews.

Activity Sheet #41
Code: I

Using Your Academic Skills Outside of School

Think about all the things you do outside of school. Do you ever use your academic skills when you're not in school? Let's find out.

> ***INSTRUCTIONS:*** Write all the academic skills you would use to perform these activities on the lines provided below. Be sure to think carefully and don't leave any skills out—your job could depend on it.

1. Make lemonade to sell.

   Skills used: ______________________________

2. Make signs advertising my product.

   Skills used: ______________________________

3. Make change when customers buy lemonade.

   Skills used: ______________________________

4. Figure out my profits.

   Skills used: ______________________________

I've Cut My Hand!

Suppose you fell and cut your hand. Then you went inside and washed the cut. Next, you put antispetic on the cut. Finally, you put a bandaid over the cut.

Why did you clean and bandage your cut? What have you learned in school that taught you cleaning a wound is important. Write your answer on the lines below.

____

____

____

____

____

____

____

■ *EXTRA ACTIVITY*—Academic Skill Breakdown

Think of some activity you do outside of school where you use your academic skills. Write the activity at the top of a separate sheet of paper. List all the academic skills you use to perform this activity on the paper.

Activity Sheet #42
Code: I

Using Your Self-Management Skills

In your *Dream Catchers* book, you learned about "self-management" skills. They included personal qualities like:

- **Good Work Habits**—A work habit is the way you do your work. Good work habits include qualities like following directions, getting work done on time, working quickly and neatly, and being prepared.
- **Good Work Attitudes**—A work attitude is how you feel about doing your work. Good work attitudes include qualities like being eager to try new tasks, working independently, sticking with hard tasks, being cheerful, accepting responsibility, and obeying rules.
- **Good Interpersonal Skills**—Interpersonal skills are how you get along with other people when doing work. Good interpersonal skills include qualities like cooperating, sharing, accepting others, respecting others, respecting authority, and being honest.

INSTRUCTIONS: Write a story about something you did where you used good self-management skills. It could be a school assignment, a chore at home, a project for girl or boy scouts, playing on a team, anything you want. Try to specifically mention all the good work habits, good work attitudes and interpersonal skills you used to complete your task.

Activity Sheet #43
Code: I

Improving Your Self-Management Skills

On page 30 in your *Dream Catchers* book you gave yourself "marks" on your self-management skills. Look at the marks you gave yourself that were either "I" or "X." These are the areas where you need to improve—starting now!

> ***INSTRUCTIONS:*** One way to start improving on something is to set goals for improvement. The steps below will get you started on these goals.

1. Select one self-management skill you want to improve. Write it on the chart below.
2. List five rules for yourself that will help you improve this skill. Write them on the chart below.
3. Tape this chart to the inside top of your desk or keep it in a notebook.
4. Each week for four weeks, grade yourself on how you followed your rules. Use the same marking system on page 30. Put your grade in the box at the bottom of your chart. If you don't show improvement in four weeks, review your rules and start again.

SELF-MANAGEMENT SKILLS IMPROVEMENT CHART				
Skill That I Will Improve:				
Rules I Will Follow To Improve This Skill:				
1.				
2.				
3.				
4.				
5.				
Grade Yourself:	**Week #1**	**Week #2**	**Week #3**	**Week #4**
0 = Outstanding				
S = Satisfactory				
I = Improvement				
X = Unsatisfactory				

Activity Sheet #44
Code: I, 2 Pages

Using Time Efficiently in the Workplace

Using time efficiently is one of the most important qualities of a good worker. To be "efficient" means you get your work done quickly, but you still do a good job.

INSTRUCTIONS: Read Maria's story below to see why efficient workers are so important. Then solve the problems that come after the story.

Maria's House Painting Business

Maria owns Pronto Painting Company. Her company paints houses. George Liska wants Pronto Painting Co. to paint his house. Maria has to decide what to charge Mr. Liska. She judges how many hours it will take to paint his house. Then she figures out what her expenses will be to paint it. Maria has to pay salaries to her workers to paint the house. That is her biggest expense. Maria subtracts the expenses from what she will charge Mr. Liska. The money left over is her profit. She uses her profit to pay herself and to keep her business running. Maria figures out her profit by using a worksheet. Look at her worksheet below.

EXPENSE AND PROFIT WORKSHEET	
EXPENSES:	
Total number of hours needed to paint house	64 hours
Salaries for two painters at $10 per hour (64 × $10 = $640)	$ 640.00
Other Expenses:	+ 100.00
TOTAL EXPENSES:	$ 740.00
PROFIT:	
Charge to Mr. Liska to paint house	$1,200.00
Less Total Expenses:	– 740.00
TOTAL PROFIT:	$ 460.00

Can Wasting Time Waste Money?

A "cost over run" in business is when something turns out to cost more than you thought it would. Maria thought it would take 64 hours to paint Mr. Liska's house. What would happen if her painters were not efficient workers? Suppose they took a lot of breaks, forgot their tools and had to get them, and just worked slowly? What would happen if they took 74 hours to finish the painting instead of 64 hours at $10 per hour? How much money would Maria lose? Figure out her loss below:

1. Estimated profit from Maria's worksheet— $460.00
   Cost over run (10 more hours x $10.00 per hour) — –______
   Actual profit— ______
2. The cost over run on Mr. Liska's house was $100. Suppose Maria's company had 10 jobs in one month. If each job had a cost over run of $100. how much money would her company lose in a month? $ __________.
3. Maria's company works 12 months a year. What if she had a cost over run of $1,000 for 7 months in a year. How much money would her company lose in a year? $ ______________.
4. Do you think wasting time wastes money? Why?

   ____

   ____

5. If you were Maria, how would you solve the problem of your painters working too slowly?

   ____

   ____

   ____

> ***NOTE:*** One of the top three reasons people get fired from their jobs is because they don't use their work time efficiently!)

6. What does it mean to be an efficient worker?

   ____

   ____

   ____

   ____

   ____

Activity Sheet #45
Code: C

Make a School Timecard

Using time efficiently is very important in the world of work. Many business practices are connected to the idea of time. Lots of people have jobs where they use timecards to keep track of the hours they work. Frequently, people even put their time card in a machine that marks the time they get to work and the time they leave. If someone gets to work at 8:01 a.m. instead of 8 a.m. the timecard shows they were late!

INSTRUCTIONS: All businesses want workers who always get to work on time and don't miss a lot of work (leave work early or are frequently absent). To see how good a worker you are, follow the instructions below to make your own timecard.

1. Make a timecard on a small sheet of paper or an index card.
2. Put your name and the dates for one week, Monday through Friday, at the top of your timecard. For example: Kate Lindsay, November 20—25, 1992
3. Make two columns underneath your name and date. One should say "Time In." The other should say "Time Out."
4. Write the days of the week along the left hand margin for Monday through Friday.
5. Make an envelope to keep your timecard in. Fold a piece of paper in half. The fold will be the top. Tape the sides and bottom of the paper to your desk. (The inside top would be a good place.) Keep your timecard in the envelope.
6. Your teacher will tell you a time when all students have to be at their desks in the morning ready to work. For example: 9 a.m.
7. At 9 a.m., your teacher will say, "Sign in please." If you are at your desk, put "9:00" under the "Time In" column. If you are not at your desk ready to sign in, write "Late."
8. Follow the same procedure for signing out early and leaving school at the end of the day.
9. If you are absent, make sure to mark that on your timecard when you return to school.
10. At the end of the week, make a record of the number of times you were on time, late and absent. Make a new timecard for the next week. Use your timecard for a whole grading period (or even the whole year). You will find out if you are the kind of prompt worker someone would like to hire.

Activity Sheet #46
Code: I

The Case of the "Bad Worker"

Unfortunately, not all workers have good work habits, good work attitudes or good interpersonal skills. When someone has to work with a person who has bad self-management skills, it can affect everyone in the workplace. Perhaps you have even had to do some task with a person who wouldn't cooperate or didn't do his or her fair share of the work. You know that wasn't a pleasant experience. To find out how "bad workers" can affect other workers, do the activity below.

> ***INSTRUCTIONS:*** Select someone you know who works at a part- or full-time job. It can be an older brother or sister, a parent, guardian, relative or neighbor. Ask them the following questions and take careful notes so you can write a report. Use the back of this sheet to record your notes. Share your report with your classmates.

1. Did you ever have to work with someone who did not have good work habits, attitudes or interpersonal skills?

> ***NOTE:*** You can write down the definitions for each of the above from your *Dream Catchers* book to show to the person you're talking with.

2. What bad work habits, work attitudes, or interpersonal skills did this person display?
3. How did her or his behavior affect other workers?
4. Did anyone ever try to "correct" this bad behavior? What happened?

Activity Sheet #47
Code: I

What Job-Related Skills Do You Need?

In your *Dream Catchers* book, you learned that workers need to learn special skills to perform their jobs. These are called "job-related" skills. In this activity you will interview someone you know. The interview will help you learn more about the job-related skills people use and how they learn them.

> ***INSTRUCTIONS:*** Select an adult you know to interview. Ask them the following questions and be sure to take good notes on what they say. You can use the back of this paper to write the answers.

1. What is your job?________________________________
2. What special skills do you need to do this work?____________________

   ____

   Name and describe some. ______________________________

   ____
3. Where did you learn the skills for your job?______________________

   ____
4. Can the skills for your job be learned in different places too? ____________

   ____

   What are the other places? ______________________________

   ____
5. Does your job require you to have any kind of academic degree? ____________

   ____

   What kind of degree?__________________________________
6. Does your job require a special license or did you have to pass a test to get it?

   ____
7. Do you have to keep learning new skills for your job? ________ Where do you learn them?

   ____

When you have finished your interview, use your notes to write a report called "The Job-Related Skills of a ____________________________ ." (Fill in the job title.) Share your report with your classmates.

Activity Sheet #48
Code: I, SG

Create a Job-Related Skills Bulletin Board

In your *Dream Catchers* book, you learned about job-related skills. They are special skills workers need to perform their jobs. Different jobs require different kinds of skills. This activity will help illustrate the differences.

> ***INSTRUCTIONS:*** Follow the steps below to learn more about the job-related skills that different jobs require.

1. Cut pictures from magazines of people working at different jobs. You can also draw pictures if you'd like.
2. For each job, make a list of all the skills you can think of that would be needed for the job. You might like to do this in a small group. Give your list a title.
3. Proofread your list to make sure all words are spelled correctly. Copy the list over if necessary to make sure it's neat.
4. Paste the picture of the job and the list of skills for that job on a piece of construction paper or poster board.
5. Decorate your bulletin boards or the walls outside your classroom with your work.

Activity Sheet #49
Code: SG, C

Using the Want Ads to Learn About Skills

Every day, your local newspaper contains "want ads." These are advertisements put in the paper by employers who want to hire people to work for them. The want ads can tell you a lot about the skills employers are looking for in workers.

INSTRUCTIONS: Reading the want ads may not be the best way to find a job, but they will tell you what employers are looking for. The Sunday paper usually has the largest want ad section. Bring the want ads to class in order to do this activity.

1. Divide the wants ads among several small groups in your class.
2. Each group will need four sheets of notebook paper. Label one sheet "Academic Skills," the second, "Self-Management Skills," the third, "Job-Related Skills," and the fourth, "Training or Education Required."
3. Read your group's want ads. Every time you find an academic, self-management, or job-related skill, or specific education or training required, write it in on the paper with that heading.
4. When all groups are done, compare what you have discovered about skills and training.

■ *EXTRA ACTIVITY*—Skills and Training List

You might want to combine each group's list into one long list for each category. Display your lists somewhere in the classroom.

Activity Sheet #50
Code: I

Write a Letter Home—Part 2

You have now finished Part 2 of your *Dream Catchers* activity book. Write a letter home explaining what you have learned.

You can use your *Dream Catchers* book for help.

INSTRUCTIONS: Write a letter home using the suggestions given below. Your teacher will explain the correct letter form, or you can look up rules for writing letters in your language book. If you decide to mail the letter, make sure you address the envelope correctly too.

Your letter should include the following information:

Paragraph 1—Give the title of your book and the section title for Part 2. (Check your language book for the correct way to write book titles and chapter titles.) Explain that you have just finished all the activities in Part 2.

Paragraph 2—Explain what academic, self-management, and job-related skills are. You might give some examples of each. Also tell how you learned that academic and self-management skills are important to do well in school and at work.

Paragraph 3—Explain that you learned about different ways you can get education and training for jobs. You might give a few examples. Tell what kind of training or education you think you'd like to have to prepare for a job.

Paragraph 4—Explain which activity you liked the most in Part 2 and why.

■ *EXTRA ACTIVITY*—Letter Exchange

Exchange letters with a classmate. Proofread one another's letter. Make sure they are written in the correct form, are punctuated correctly, and do not contain spelling errors. Write a final, corrected copy of your letter if needed.

PART 3

Making Dreams Come True—*Ability, Effort, and Achievement*

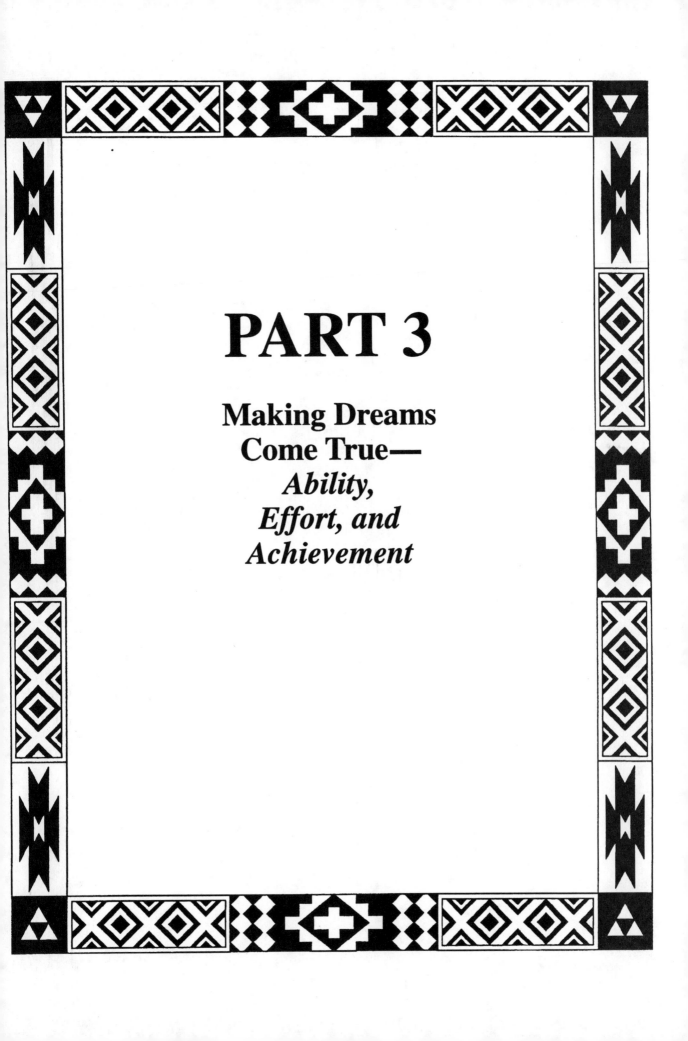

Activity Sheet #51
Code: SG, C

Produce a "Three Little Pigs" Play

Your *Dream Catchers* book contains "The Modern Fable of the Three Little Pigs." You can have a lot of fun with that story by changing it into a play you can perform. Read the instructions to see how.

INSTRUCTIONS: Plan and write a script for the "Three Little Pigs" fable. The characters you will need are:

- Narrator
- Pig I Can
- Pig I'll Try
- Pig I Did It
- The Big Bad Wolf
- Mother Pig

You can change the whole story into a script. Or you can just decide what parts of the story the narrator will read and let the characters make up what they will say based on the story as they perform. (That's called "extemporaneous theatre.") If you have time, plan and make costumes. (You can make great pig and wolf masks from brown paper bags.) Plan and make any scenery you might want to use, but keep it simple.

■ *EXTRA ACTIVITY*—Perform Pig Plays

1. If you and your classmates wrote "Which Little Pig Are You?" stories in your *Dream Catchers* book, pick the best story for each little pig. (You can select a small group of students to be judges or your teacher can pick them.) Turn those stories into plays too. You can divide your class into four groups and each group can plan and perform a play.
2. Invite other classes to your "Pig Theatre" and perform the plays for them. Do "The Modern Fable of Three Little Pigs" first and then the "Which Little Pig Are You?" plays next. You can have your audience guess which little pig was being represented in the play if you'd like.

Activity Sheet #52
Code: I

You Can Improve Too!

INSTRUCTIONS: Pick one of the subjects you identified as your weakness. (See page 49 in your *Dream Catchers* book.) Then fill in the chart below. Try to be specific with your solutions. For example: **Causes of My Problem** — I forgot to take my books home. **How Can I Improve** — Write down the books I need in an assignment notebook.

My Work Improvement Plan

NAME: ______________________________

I Need To Improve In (Name Subject): ______________________________

CAUSES OF MY PROBLEM?	**HOW I CAN IMPROVE?**
______________________________	______________________________
______________________________	______________________________
______________________________	______________________________
______________________________	______________________________
______________________________	______________________________
______________________________	______________________________
______________________________	______________________________
______________________________	______________________________
______________________________	______________________________
______________________________	______________________________
______________________________	______________________________
______________________________	______________________________
______________________________	______________________________
______________________________	______________________________
______________________________	______________________________
______________________________	______________________________
______________________________	______________________________
______________________________	______________________________

Activity Sheet #53
Code: I

My Time Journal

MY TIME JOURNAL			
Date:			
6:00 a.m.		**6:30**	
7:00		**7:30**	
8:00		**8:30**	
9:00		**9:30**	
10:00		**10:30**	
11:00		**11:30**	
12:00 p.m.		**12:30 p.m.**	
1:00		**1:30**	
2:00		**2:30**	
3:00		**3:30**	
4:00		**4:30**	
5:00		**5:30**	
6:00		**6:30**	
7:00		**7:30**	
8:00		**8:30**	
9:00		**9:30**	
10:00		**10:30**	
11:00		**11:30**	
12:00 A.M.			

Activity Sheet #54
Code: I

How You Use Your Time

When you did your "Time Journal" in your *Dream Catchers* book, you categorized all your activities for the week and added up the number of hours you spent on each activity. Many times in business, people put information on charts and graphs so it's easier to make comparisons and see information. Use the information you gathered to make a bar chart of your activities and the time you spent on them.

INSTRUCTIONS: Write your activities at the bottom of the graph. Use a marker or ink pen to draw bars up to the number of hours you spent on each activity.

Hours

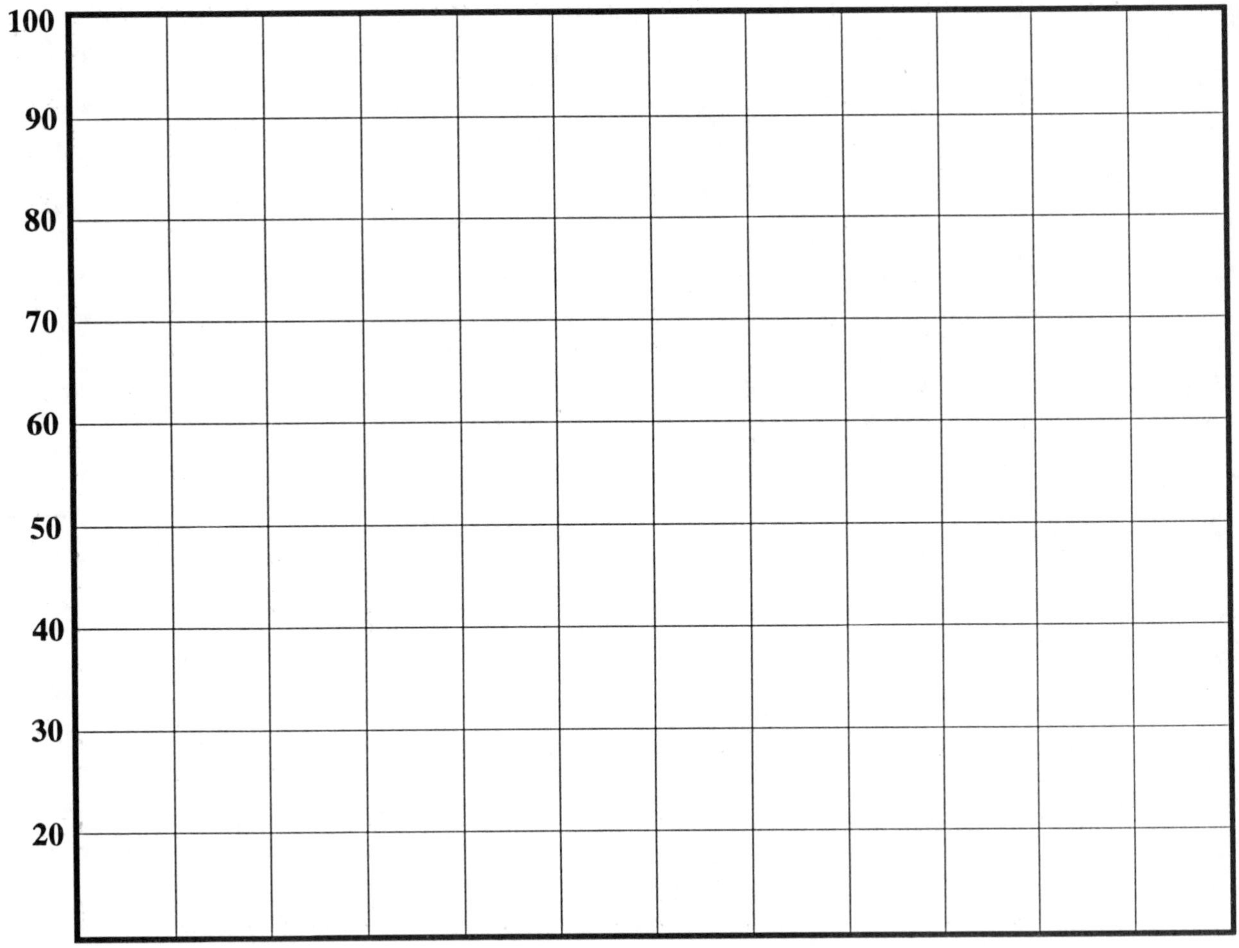

Activity:

Activity Sheet #55
Code: I

Setting Achievement Goals

You know a lot now about your weaknesses and how you spend your time. You can use that information to improve your school work. Use your "Work Improvement Plan" and your "Time Journal" in your *Dream Catchers* book to help set achievement goals.

> ***INSTRUCTIONS:*** Fill in the goal plan below. Your teacher may want you to copy your goals on a separate sheet of paper. You can take your goal plan home and show your parent(s) or guardian(s). They can help you reach your goals. Good luck!

MY ACHIEVEMENT GOALS

Goal #1: My study time during the week will be between ______ p.m. and ______ p.m.

Goal #2: On weekends, I will study on . . . (give day and times).

____

Goal #3: I will spend more time on these subjects (your weaknesses) ________________

____

Goal #4: On weekdays, I plan to be in bed with the lights out by ______________ each night.

Goal #5: I will only watch TV and movies or play video games for __________ hour(s) on weekdays and __________ hours on weekends.

Activity Sheet #56
Code: I

Make a Schoolwork Planner

INSTRUCTIONS: To help you organize your time and schoolwork to make sure everything gets done, use the "Weekly Planner" below. Make sure to use one each week.

MY WEEKLY SCHOOLWORK PLANNER

Activity	Monday	Tuesday	Wednesday	Thursday	Friday	Weekend
Books and Supplies To Bring Home						
Work Due Tomorrow						
Tests Coming up						
Subjects To Review						
Times To Study						
Other Things I Have To Do Today						

Activity Sheet #57
Code: I

Managing Your School Study Time

Sometimes your teacher gives you time during the school day to study. Do you use that time efficiently? Do you get your work done in the time your teacher gives you?

INSTRUCTIONS: Take the quiz below to find out how you manage your study time at school. Circle the correct answer and read the answer key to find out your score.

STUDY TIME QUIZ

Statement	Yes	No
1. It usually takes me at least five minutes to get my materials together to start studying, for example book, paper, and pencil		
2. I frequently need to borrow paper or a pencil from classmates before I start studying.		
3. My desk is a mess most of the time.		
4. I often sharpen my pencil during study time.		
5. Sometimes I write notes to my friends during study time.		
6. I look at the clock or my watch at least four times when I'm studying.		
7. I often think, "I'll just take this home and do it" instead of getting my work done in school.		
8. I like to talk with people sitting near me when I'm studying.		
9. I like to look out the window during study time.		
10. I always seem to be rushing to get my work done.		
11. I like to read other things during study time instead of doing my assignment.		

ANSWER KEY: If you had more than four "Yes" answers, you need to use your school study time more efficiently. You should probably do the activity sheet on setting study goals for school.

Activity Sheet #58
Code: I

Using School Study Time Better

Your "Managing Study Time at School" quiz can help you identify the weaknesses in your study habits. Look over all your "Yes" answers and decide how you are wasting most of your time. Follow the instructions below to turn your weaknesses into strengths.

INSTRUCTIONS: Set three goals for yourself on the worksheet below to help improve your study skills. Tape your goal plan to your inside desk cover or somewhere you can easily see it. When you have study time at school, quickly read your goals. When study time is over, ask yourself if you used your time efficiently.

MY SCHOOL STUDY TIME GOALS

Goal #1: ______________________________

____

____

Goal #2: ______________________________

____

____

Goal #3: ______________________________

____

____

Activity Sheet #59
Code: SG, C

"A Test Is Coming!"

The grade you get on a test very often reflects how efficient you are in studying for a test. Do you study the "right" things? Do you plan your study time wisely? Do you have all the materials you need to study? Do you follow your teacher's instructions? Do you spend enough time studying?

INSTRUCTIONS: Work in small groups to "brainstorm" better ways to help you prepare for tests. Follow the steps below for guidance on how to create a worksheet designed to help you study.

1. Make a list of all the different things you should do to study for a test. Your list should apply to all your subjects. When brainstorming, you put down everything you can possibly think of at first.
2. Look at your list and see if you can put the different items into categories—like putting things in clusters. Reading, reviewing, and materials might be some of your clusters.
3. Organize your clusters in priority order. What is the most important thing to do? What is second, third, or fourth?
4. Organize the items in your clusters in priority order. At this point you may choose to throw out some of your items or combine them.
5. Compare your group's clusters with other groups. Add anything to your lists that other groups had but you didn't. If groups have different priorities, you may discuss those differences and decide who is "right."
6. Write a final copy of your clusters and their items in priority order. Make it a worksheet "checklist" so any student using your worksheet to prepare for a test can "check off" the items as they finish them.
7. See if someone in your group can type your checklist. Have your teacher run off copies for everyone. Use your checklist every time you have a test.

Activity Sheet #60
Code: I

Learn from Your Mistakes

Imagine that you are looking at a glass that is half-filled with water. How would you describe the glass of water? Would you say it is "half-empty" or "half-full?" "Half-empty" is a negative way of looking at things and "half-full" is positive.

If you took a test and got half the questions wrong, you'd get a very bad grade, of course. But the positive side is that you also got half the questions right! If you got half right, you can get more right if you try.

INSTRUCTIONS: This activity is designed to help you analyze your test-taking skills. You CAN improve your test grades! Follow the steps below.

1. When you get a test back look at your wrong answers. Then look up the right answers and correct your test. If it's a math test, redo the problems to get the right answers.
2. Look at the answers you got wrong. On a separate sheet of paper, write a reason for why you got each answer wrong. You may write the same reason several times. Be specific when stating your reasons. For example:
   - I made a stupid mistake. (You knew the right answer but marked it wrong on the test.)
   - I misunderstood the question.
   - I didn't study that part of the chapter.
   - I didn't know how to do the problem.
   - I forgot the answer.
3. Look at the reasons why you made mistakes on your test. Which reason did you give most frequently? That's the area you most need to work on when studying and taking tests.
4. Write some rules for yourself to avoid making these mistakes in the future. For example, if you said, "I made a stupid mistake," your rule might be, "Read test questions carefully and check my answers when I'm done." You might want to add these rules to your "A Test Is Coming!" worksheet. If they're already on the worksheet, put a star by them to remind you to really work on those study skills. Use your new knowledge every time you study for a test.

Activity Sheet #61
Code: I

My Workplace Plan

INSTRUCTIONS: Fill in the blanks below to design your study workplace. Take your plan home and show it to your parent(s) or guardian(s). They can help you organize and use your workplace.

1. Where will I work? (You need a desk or table, good lighting, and a quiet place.)

____

____

2. What supplies will I need? (List everything you should have for all subjects.)

____

____

3. Where will I keep my supplies? (A desk drawer is great. A shoe box or some other container will also work. Plan a place to keep your supplies.)

____

____

4. How can I remember to bring home the books I need?

____

____

5. What "study rules" should I follow? (You need quiet and no interruptions from people, the phone, or TV, to concentrate best. Get snacks before you start. Write your rules.)

____

____

6. Who will I study with? (Most of the time, it's more efficient to study alone. List the times when it would be O.K. to study with friends.)

____

____

Workplace Plan

Activity Sheet #62
Code: I, SG, C, 2 Pages

Organizing an Efficient Workplace

Sometimes where you work can make you an inefficient worker. ("Inefficient" is the opposite of "efficient.") A well-organized workplace is very important in the world of work. Businesses want to make sure the workplace is designed so workers won't waste time getting their work done. Sometimes they even hire special people called "consultants" to design the most efficient workplace possible. Read Willy's story below to see how where you work can make a difference.

Can You Help Willy?

The Richards family owns a doughnut shop. Willy Richards comes in at 4 a.m. every day to make the doughnuts. Willy loves his work, but he is unhappy with his kitchen. He thinks he wastes a lot of time walking back and forth because of the way the kitchen is organized. Willy has to work long hours. Wasting time cuts down on the profit the doughnut shop earns. Willy decides he wants to change the kitchen to make it a more efficient workplace. Then he can make the doughnuts in less time which will mean more profit for the family.

INSTRUCTIONS: The list below tells you all the steps to make doughnuts. The next page shows you a floor plan of Willy's kitchen and how it is organized. Look at the floor plan and pretend you are Willy. Go through each step to make the doughnuts. You can draw arrows or footsteps on the floor plan to show all the walking Willy has to do. Does Willy waste time walking back and forth?

Steps for Making Doughnuts

1. Get the following items and bring them to the worktable:
   - baking supplies (flour, sugar, etc.)
   - baking utensils (bowls, spoons, etc.)
   - milk
2. Mix the batter for the doughnuts on the worktable.
3. Take the batter to the doughnut maker and pour it in.
4. Get the baking pans and bring them to the doughnut maker. Make doughnuts.
5. Put doughnuts in the oven.
6. Take baked doughnuts out of the oven and put them on the cooling racks.
7. Bring cooled doughnuts to the worktable to frost them.
8. Put all dirty baking utensils and pans in the sink when done.

Floor Plan of Willy's Kitchen

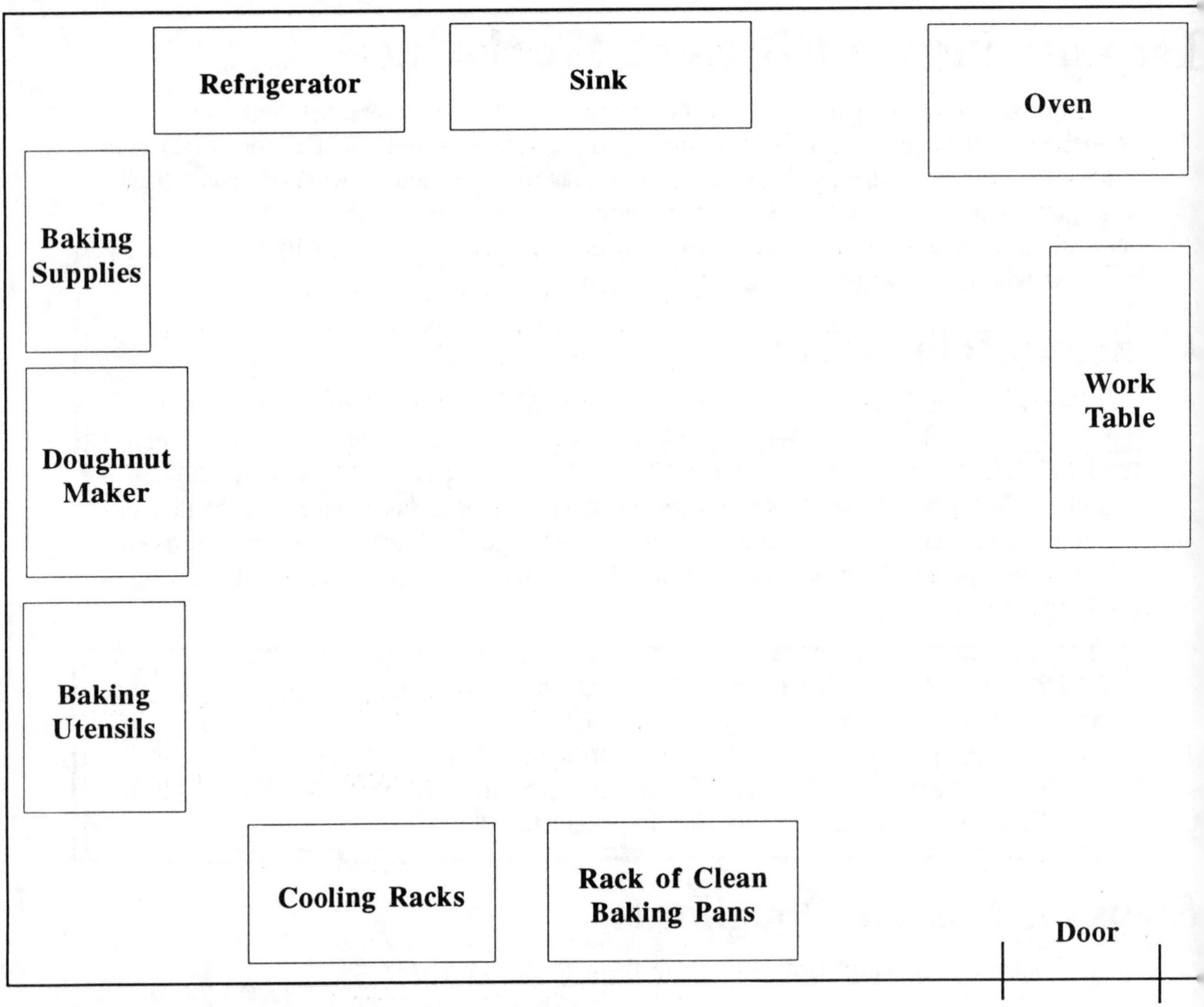

You Can Be Willy's Consultant

> ***INSTRUCTIONS:*** Get a blank sheet of paper and a ruler and draw a 5 × 6 inch rectangle. Draw a new floor plan for Willy's kitchen to help him save time. You might need to try several before you get the best design. The floor plan should include: 1) a place for baking supplies; 2) a place for baking utensils; 3) a sink; 4) a refrigerator; 5) a worktable; 6) a doughnut maker; 7) an oven; 8) a place for clean baking pans, and 9) cooling racks.

You might do this in small groups. Compare your floor plans to other plans and vote on which one is the best. You could also "set up" each group's kitchen design in the classroom using desks to represent the kitchen furniture. Then you could actually count the steps needed in each plan to see which one is the best.

Activity Sheet #63
Code: C

Improving Your School Workplace

In your *Dream Catchers* book, you did an activity to help you improve the organization of your workplace at home. But the classroom and your desk are also your workplace. Your class and teacher can analyze the schoolroom workplace and think of ways to improve it.

> *INSTRUCTIONS:* Select one day to be your "Workplace Analysis" day and try to think of ways to improve the efficiency of your class workplace. Brainstorm in small groups and write answers to the suggestions listed below. Then discuss your suggestions as a class. Establish workplace rules and policies. All businesses have them.

1. **Your desk**—Your desk is personal and everyone will not organize his or her desk in the same way. Yet, try to think of some general rules for keeping books and supplies easy to get to. Also, you might consider how frequently and when desks should be cleaned.
2. **Old homework papers, worksheets, and tests**—These papers are all excellent sources for study and review for tests. But most students throw them away or lose them. Can you develop a classroom filing system so everyone has a place to file and save their papers? Keeping track of paperwork is extremely important in businesses.
3. **Desk arrangement**—How are your desks arranged? Does the arrangement make it easier or harder to do your work? Can you think of different arrangements you might try to make your classroom a more efficient place to work?
4. **Seat assignments**—How are seats assigned? Do you constantly talk to the people sitting next to you? Can you sit near your friends and resist the temptation to talk? What might be the best way to assign seats?
5. **Quiet time**—Certain times during the day may be assigned as "quiet time," for study, homework, or reading. How should "quiet time" be announced? Should you have a sign or signal like ringing a bell? What rules should be observed during "quiet time?" For example, can you sharpen your pencil? What should happen to classmates who do not follow "quiet time" rules? People who do not follow the rules often get fired at work because they disrupt the efficiency of other workers.
6. **Rules and Policies**—Once you establish your workplace rules and policies, review them every few months to see if they are working. If not, identify the problems and revise your rules.

Activity Sheet #64
Code: C

Developing a Job Chart

Every classroom has certain tasks that need to be done to keep it orderly such as cleaning the boards, watering plants or feeding pets. Since the classroom is your workplace, everyone should be responsible for keeping it orderly.

> *INSTRUCTIONS:* You can develop a job chart for keeping order in your classroom. Simply follow the steps below.

1. In class discussion, make a list of all the tasks that need to be accomplished each day and once a week.
2. Have one or two students volunteer to make a job chart for the classroom tasks. The job chart should contain:
   - A "Supervisor" heading
   - A daily task list
   - A weekly task list

   Each task will have an index card with a student's name on it placed next to it. So be sure to leave enough space between each task for the card to fit.
3. Have a few students volunteer to write all students' names on index cards.
4. Hang your job chart on a bulletin board.
5. All students should take turns performing tasks in a rotating order. How to make a sample task list is outlined below.

Assigning Work

1. Take the index cards with the students' names on them. Pin one name next to "supervisor" and pin other names next to each task. Store the remaining cards in a safe place.
2. The supervisor is responsible for checking to see that jobs are done, and doing the job of anyone who is absent.
3. At the end of the day on Friday, the supervisor takes down the name cards and puts them on the bottom of the name card deck. He or she then assigns new workers for the next week. Take the cards from the top of the deck and pin them on the job chart.
4. If the supervisor is absent on Friday, the person whose name is next on the job chart will assign next week's tasks.

Activity Sheet #65
Code: I

Write a Letter Home—Part 3

You have now finished Part 3 of your *Dream Catchers* activity book. Write a letter home explaining what you have learned.

You can use your *Dream Catchers* book for help.

INSTRUCTIONS: Write a letter home using the suggestions given below. Your teacher will explain the correct letter form, or you can look up rules for writing letters in your Language book. If you decide to mail the letter, make sure you address the envelope correctly too.

Your letter should include the following information:

Paragraph 1—Give the title of your book and the section title for Part 3. (Check your language book for the correct way to write book titles and chapter titles.) Explain that you have just finished all the activities in Part 3.

Paragraph 2—Explain that you have been learning ways to improve your study skills. Tell how you wrote a work improvement plan to help you improve in a subject (name the subject).

Paragraph 3—Explain about your time journal and what you discovered about how you use your time. Explain that your time journal helped you establish study rules and achievement goals for yourself. You might give a few examples of your rules or goals.

Paragraph 4—Explain what your learned about the relationship between ability, effort and achievement.

Paragraph 5—Tell which activity you like best in Part 3 and why.

■ *EXTRA ACTIVITY*—Letter Exchange

Exchange letters with a classmate. Proofread one another's letter. Make sure they are written in the correct form, are punctuated correctly, and do not contain spelling errors. Write a final, corrected copy of your letter if needed.

PART 4

Putting Your Dreams to Work—*Work and the Needs and Functions of Society*

Activity Sheet #66
Code: I, C

Why Do People Work?

You might think the answer to the question is "for money." It's true people do need money for food, shelter and clothing. But if people only worked for money, everyone would just try to get jobs that really paid a lot of money. And all people don't do that. People also work for the satisfaction they get from their jobs. Since people are different, what satisfies them is different too. Follow the instructions below to learn more about why people work.

INSTRUCTIONS: You and your classmates are going to do a survey about why people work. A good person to start with is your teacher.

1. Ask your teacher the following question: "What satisfaction do you get from your work?" List three things in priority order. (#1 is the most important.)
2. Each class member should ask five other people that question and bring the answers to class. (Remember working at home is also a job.) Make sure to list the most important reason first. It might be fun to ask another teacher to see if his or her response is different from your teacher.
3. When you have completed your survey, make one big list of all the answers you got. Mark the number of times people gave that answer as their #1, their #2, and their #3 priority.
4. Bring your list to class and combine all answers into one big list. That should give you a good idea of all the different reasons people work. You might take your list and hang it on the bulletin board.

■ EXTRA ACTIVITY—Job Satisfaction

Write a paragraph where you explain the kinds of satisfaction you want to get from a job when you are an adult. Do you think these reasons will be important when you select the career you want to pursue?

Activity Sheet #67
Code: I, C

Why Do You Work?

Your "job" right now is to be a student and do your schoolwork. Do students have different reasons for doing their work just like adults on the job? Let's find out by surveying your class.

> ***INSTRUCTIONS:*** To make sure everyone will feel free to put down how they really feel, do not put your name on the paper you will be asked to do.

1. On a separate sheet of paper, list in priority order (the most important first) all the reasons why you do your work in school. Write down as many as you can think of.
2. Collect everyone's lists and make one big class list of why people do their schoolwork. Mark the number of times people gave each reason as #1, #2, and #3.
3. Compare the class's reasons to the reasons given on your survey of adult workers. Are some of the reasons the same? Which ones are different? Discuss your findings.

Activity Sheet #68
Code: I, SG

Work and Society

Although people have many different jobs and many different reasons for working, everybody's job is important. People in society depend on the work done by other people. For example, if a farmer didn't plant his crops, we wouldn't have food to eat. Or if the refuse workers didn't collect the garbage, our environment would be extremely messy and an unhealthy place to live.

To show how people in society are dependent on one another to do their work, follow the instructions below.

> ***INSTRUCTIONS:*** You can do this activity alone or in small groups. You are going to take a product and think of all the workers who are involved in getting that product to you. Since everybody wears cotton T-shirts a lot, we will use that as our product.

1. Pretend that you have just purchased a cotton T-shirt that has some design on the front of it. On a separate sheet of paper, list all the workers and jobs you can think of who had a part in getting that product to you. Really brainstorm and write down as many jobs as you can.
2. Look at your list and put the work in chronological order. ("Chronological" means to put in order by time, what had to be done first, second, etc.)
3. Get a big sheet of paper and draw a big circle on it. You are going to make a pie chart on it to show the cycle of your product—what was done first, second, etc. Count the number of workers and jobs you have on your list. Divide your "pie" (the circle) into "pieces" so you will have a "piece" for each job on your list.
4. Working clockwise, write the worker and job in each pie piece. You can add illustrations if you have room.
5. Compare your pie chart to other group's pie charts. See who thought of the most jobs and workers.

■ *EXTRA ACTIVITY*—Product Pie Chart

Have each group select another product and do a pie chart to show a product cycle from its beginning to someone purchasing it. You might want to do some library research to help you get all the jobs involved.

Activity Sheet #69
Code: I, SG

What Would Happen If....

Another way to understand how people in society depend on other people to do their jobs is to think what would happen if people didn't do their jobs. Follow the instructions below to find out.

> ***INSTRUCTIONS:*** In the left-hand column below, list all the different kinds of jobs people work at in your school. In the right-hand column, write what would happen if those workers did not come to school one day.

WORKERS IN MY SCHOOL	WHAT WOULD HAPPEN IF......

Activity Sheet #70
Code: I, SG

On Strike!

Sometimes workers in our society go on strike. This means that they stop doing their work because they are dissatisfied with their working conditions. Some workers have jobs that are so important to the well-being of society that it's against the law for them to go on strike. Follow the instructions below to discover what kinds of jobs are vital to our society.

INSTRUCTIONS: In the left-hand column below list all the jobs that you think the worker's shouldn't go on strike. (Where the strike would have a very serious effect on everyone.) In the middle column, write what would happen if those workers did strike. Also, check the column if you think it's against the law for these workers to strike.

WORKERS IN SOCIETY	WHAT WOULD HAPPEN IF THESE WORKERS WENT ON STRIKE?	AGAINST THE LAW?

Activity Sheet #71
Code: I, SG

What Are Goods and Services?

Some people have jobs where they make things, like cars, a loaf of bread, a pair of shoes, a TV etc. We call these things "goods." Other people have jobs where they don't make things but help people by doing something for them. For example, repair a car, clean clothes, cut someone's hair, or sell a pair of shoes. We call these activities providing "services." Follow the instructions below to learn more about goods and services.

INSTRUCTIONS: You can do this activity by yourself or in a small group. You will need a telephone book for research purposes.

1. Look at the part of the phone book where businesses advertise. They are usually the "Yellow Pages."
2. Use two pieces of your own paper. Write "Goods" at the top of one sheet of paper and "Services" at the top of the other sheet.
3. Read the "Yellow Pages" of the phone book and make a list of the goods produced by businesses and the services offered. If you are doing this in small groups, you may want to divide the pages of the "Yellow Pages," have one group do "A through E," one group do "I through P," and the last group "Q through Z."
4. Compare your lists with other group's lists to see all the different kinds of goods and services that exist in our economy.

■ *EXTRA ACTIVITY*—Want Ad Research

Instead of using the phone book for research, you can use the want ad section of the newspaper, or use both.

Activity Sheet #72
Code: I, SG

Services for Your Home

Your home is a place that requires a lot of servicing. For example, think of the things that might break that need to be fixed. Other things beside repair work might also require the services of workers. Follow the instructions below to discover all the service jobs required to keep a home running.

INSTRUCTIONS: People hire a lot of other people to perform services for their home. In the left-hand column, make a list of all the kinds of service work you can think of that a home might require. If you can think of a job title for the person who would perform that work, write it in the right-hand column.

SERVICE NEEDED FOR A HOUSE	JOB TITLE

Activity Sheet #73
Code: I, SG

Where Do Goods Come From?

People in our society depend on workers all across the United States. Many of the goods that you use and buy are made in different states. Sometimes the raw materials needed to make a good come from one state and the product is made in another. Every state has certain goods or raw materials that they produce. Do the following activity to discover what they are.

INSTRUCTIONS: Select one or more states. If you are working in groups, you might want to take a few. Your teacher can help you decide which states to choose. Use your social studies book and/or an encyclopedia to help you do research.

1. Research your state or states to discover what products or raw materials they are known for producing.
2. Get a large piece of paper and draw a map of the state. Write the goods and raw materials that state produces on your map. You might want to draw illustrations on the map too.
3. Share the results of your research with your class. You may want to make a bulletin board with everyone's maps.

Activity Sheet #74
Code: I, C

The Global Economy

Our world and the work we do is changing. Now we entering into a time where goods are produced in a "global economy." What does that mean? It means that now we not only get goods and raw materials from different states, but more and more we get them from different countries all over the world. The following activity will help you discover more about the "global economy." It might also improve your geography skills!

INSTRUCTIONS: Follow the steps below to learn about the global economy.

Materials Needed

- straight pins
- tape
- small pieces of paper
- world map on a bulletin board

1. At home, look at different goods in your house and read the tags and labels to discover where they came from. You can look at clothes, food items, furniture, or anything that has information on where it was made.
2. Make a list of 10 items and where they were made. (You do not have to find 10 different items.) You may have, for example, several articles of clothing. But try to use as many different kinds of things as you can. Bring your list to school.
3. Using straight pins, paper, and tape, make small flags. Each flag should have the name of your product on it, for example, "shoes." Each student should make ten flags.
4. Take turns to put your flags on the world map. Put each product flag in the country where the product was made.
5. Have someone read the names of all the products made in different countries. Discuss what you discover. What have you learned about the "global economy?"

Activity Sheet #75
Code: I, SG

Goods from Around the World

You have learned that people in our society now depend on workers all across the world. Many of the goods that you use and buy are made in different countries. Sometimes the raw materials needed to make a good come from one country and the product is made in another country. Different countries have certain goods or raw materials that they produce. Do the following activity to discover what they are.

INSTRUCTIONS: Select one country to research. Your teacher can help you decide which country to choose. Use your social studies book and/or an encyclopedia to help you do research.

1. Research your country to discover what products or raw materials they are known for producing. Try to find out if they make goods that people in the United States buy. What other countries does your country sell their goods to?
2. Get a large piece of paper and draw a map of your country. Write the goods and raw materials that country produces on your map. You might want to draw illustrations on the map too.
3. Write a short report to attach to your map. Explain what countries your country sells goods to.
4. Display your maps in the classroom.

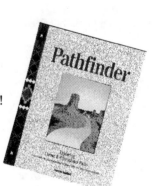

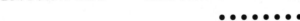

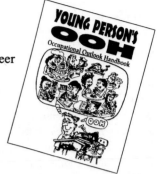

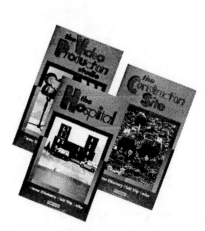

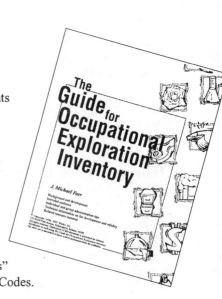

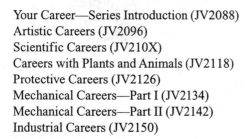

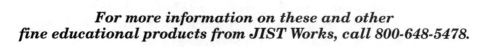